The Work of His Hands

To the Hendricks,
Blessings!

The Work of His Hands

A View of God's Creation from Space

J Williams
Ps 19

Colonel Jeffrey N. Williams

CONCORDIA PUBLISHING HOUSE · SAINT LOUIS

Published by Concordia Publishing House
3558 S. Jefferson Ave., St. Louis, MO 63118-3968
1-800-325-3040 • www.cph.org

All images courtesy of the National Aeronautics and Space Administration. See page 174 for additional photo information.

The research cited and the observations expressed in *The Work of His Hands* are those of the author, not of the National Aeronautics and Space Administration.

Cover image, ISS013-E-88243
Back cover image, ISS013-E-07987

The quote on page 77 is from Johann Wolfgang von Goethe, "Wilhelm Meisters Lehrjahre," in *Goethes Sämmtliche Werke*, vol. 7 (Stuttgart: J. G. Cotta, 1874), p. 520.

Manufactured in China

Library of Congress Cataloging-in-Publication Data

Williams, Jeffrey N.
    The work of His hands : a view of God's creation from space / Jeffrey N. Williams.
      p. cm.
    Includes bibliographical references.
    ISBN 978-0-7586-1589-3
    1. Creation--Christianity. 2. Williams, Jeffrey N.--Christianity. 3. International Space
      Station--Christianity. I. Title.

BT695.W566 2010
231.7'652--dc22
                                              2009051650

1 2 3 4 5 6 7 8 9 10   19 18 17 16 15 14 13 12 11 10

"An excellent wife is the crown of her husband." *Proverbs 12:4*

"She is far more precious than jewels. The heart of her husband trusts in her, and he will have no lack of gain. She does him good, and not harm, all the days of her life." *Proverbs 31:10–12*

This work is dedicated to Anna-Marie—my beloved wife of twenty-nine years and mother of our two sons—whom I love and adore and who has consistently loved and supported me selflessly and sacrificially while enduring many long periods of separation during military deployments, training and mission preparation, as well as spaceflights. The blessing of her companionship, partnership, love, and devotion has been a gift from God, to whom I am grateful. Anna-Marie has been and continues to be my greatest earthly provision. She truly is my Proverbs 31 bride.

Contents

Foreword

O LORD, our Lord, how majestic is Your name in all the earth! You have set Your glory above the heavens. . . . When I look at Your heavens, the work of Your fingers, the moon and the stars, which You have set in place, what is man that You are mindful of him?　　Psalm 8:1, 3–4

David wrote Psalm 8 while gazing into the night sky. He probably penned that song as an adolescent, while tending his father's flocks in some remote field. As he pondered the vast expanse of the heavens and the orderly nature of such an immense universe, he was awestruck by the realization that God, who created so many amazing wonders, is even greater, more glorious, and wiser than all of them combined.

While he was thinking about that, David was overwhelmed by the relative insignificance of humanity. He marveled that God had shown so much grace and kindness to the human race. After all, God has revealed Himself to us not only *implicitly* (in the glory of His creation) but also *explicitly* (in His Word), and above all, *personally* through the incarnation of Christ. That is the prophetic subject matter of Psalm 8, according to Hebrews 2:6–9. The idea that the Creator of the universe would thus stoop to redeem fallen creatures elicited from David a profound outpouring of pure praise.

Anyone who takes time to study the heavens can appreciate David's amazement at the spectacle. Even without a telescope or satellite photos, David could see that the glory of the universe was beyond the ability of human language to describe.

As a matter of fact, you can look from any perspective at any portion of creation, great or small, and the message built into every aspect of it is exactly the same: God's invisible attributes—namely, His eternal power and divine nature—are clearly perceptible in the things He has made. That has been true since the very beginning of creation (Romans 1:20).

Only recently however, has it been possible to study earth from heaven's perspective. Colonel Jeffrey Williams has had the rare privilege of doing just that, and the experience likewise impressed him with the greatness, glory, and grace of God, who "made heaven and earth, the sea, and all that is in them, who keeps faith forever" (Psalm 146:6).

During his six-month mission at the International Space Station in 2006, Jeff orbited the earth more than 2,800 times. He worked on hundreds of experiments while suspended in microgravity. He walked in space twice (spending more than twelve hours hanging by a tether in the atmospheric void outside the spacecraft). And while doing all that, he took more photographs of the earth than any astronaut in history.

In a journal entry written from the International Space Station and posted on a NASA Web site near the end of his first month in orbit, Jeff wrote:

> Another activity that we really enjoy is earth photography or what we formally call "earth observation."
>
> You can never tire of looking at the part of God's creation we call Earth. Traveling around the globe every 90 minutes provides lots of opportunity to view the geography, oceans, cloud formations, sunrises and sunsets, thunderstorms, city lights, and many other things in vivid detail.

Jeff preserved, as much as possible, that vivid detail in an amazing collection of stunning digital photographs.

I was privileged to see some of Jeff's photography almost immediately via e-mail while he was still in orbit. One shot that especially stands out in my mind is an extraordinary view of California from above, with the coastline mostly obscured by a massive smoke plume from the sixth largest wildfire in California history. Known as the Day Fire, it burned out of control for nearly the entire month of September 2006. For several days, that smoke plume permeated and overshadowed the community where I live and minister. But a photograph of the fire from orbit is what enabled me to appreciate the true size of the fire—and the amazing mercy seen in the fact that not a single life was lost in it.

That was just one snapshot. Every view from the window of the International Space Station contains countless vivid lessons about the meticulous goodness of Divine Providence, God's care for His creation, and His wisdom in ordering the universe. Jeff Williams has a wonderful gift for seeing those things and pointing them out.

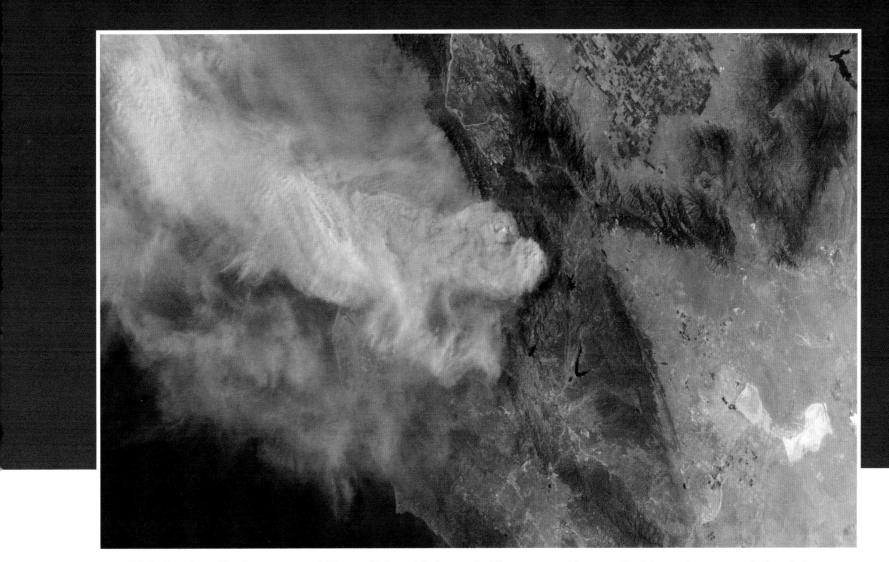

This book tells the story of Expedition 13 from Jeff's perspective as flight engineer—while giving us a front-row seat in the Space Station and letting us look through the lens of his camera. Jeff's photos and written descriptions are filled with graphic reminders about the greatness and power of God, our own relative insignificance, and the great mercy whereby God cares for us.

Get ready for your thoughts to be transported to heaven and your heart to be lifted in praise. You are about to enjoy a spectacular perspective on our Creator, our world, and our place in the universe in a way you probably never have carefully considered before.

John MacArthur, pastor
Grace Community Church, Sun Valley, CA

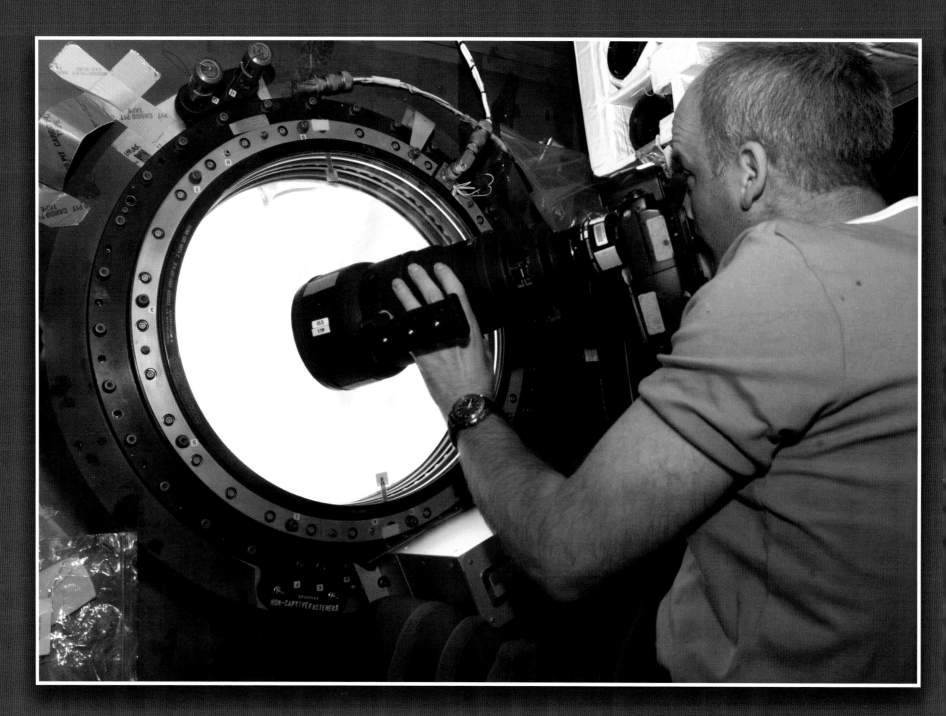

Capturing observations of the Earth below through handheld photography, Williams steadies himself at the window of the ISS's Destiny module.

Preface

The world will never starve for want of wonders; but only for want of wonder.
—G. K. Chesterton, *Tremendous Trifles*

What is the biggest highlight of spaceflight? I receive this question frequently. It is a difficult—perhaps impossible—question to answer in the singular. There are so many highlights, and the one that bubbles to the top at a given moment varies.

The biggest highlight could be a space walk or a singular moment of a space walk, a grand view of a particular feature of the earth, or a sunset; the launch, entry, or landing; the rendezvous and docking; or perhaps the arrival of visitors during a long expedition. All of these experiences and many others compete for the top position. Each time I consider the question, many highlights bubble around in my memory continuously being replaced by another. So the question can never really be answered if I only consider the tangible events and experiences of the journey.

But I can answer it—and often do—in another way. The single most rewarding highlight of spaceflight is bringing the experience to others and vicariously taking them along on the journey. That includes you, the reader. It is my hope that this book allows you to experience and enjoy some of those many highlights I have experienced. Perhaps, in a small way, it will inspire you beyond your current horizons or help you inspire others beyond theirs. That is the purpose of this book.

Welcome aboard!

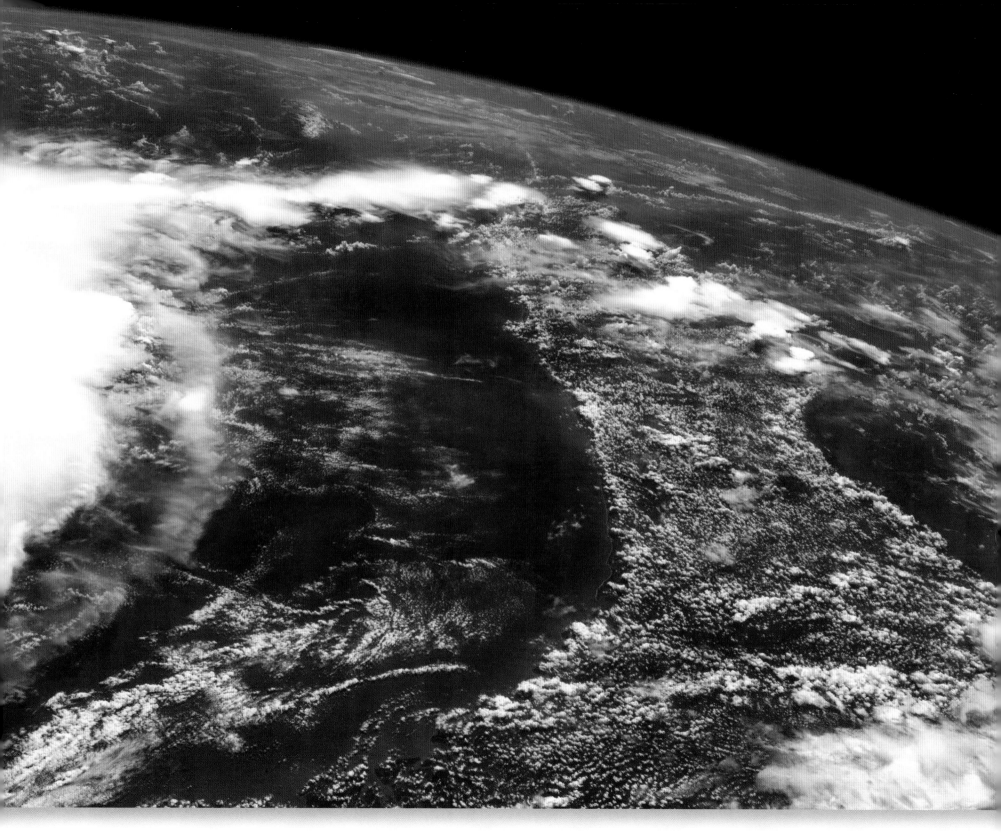

14   Oblique view of the Florida Peninsula.

Acknowledgments

Many people have directly contributed to making this book possible, and I am greatly indebted to them.

Ultimately, the most visible record of space exploration is the photography. The photography contained within this book would not have been possible were it not for the dedication and hard work of the Earth Observation scientists as well as the photography training team in preparing flight crews for the task of capturing the images. The quality and quantity of photography using the very complex equipment on board the International Space Station was a direct result of their commitment and professionalism. (See page 174, "About the Photographs," for information on the camera equipment used. There you will also find links to the NASA Web sites that feature more incredible pictures.)

The entire Expedition 13 training, flight control, support, and management teams were responsible for a smooth, efficient, successful, and safe flight, making the opportunity for the photography possible. Their participation and enthusiasm in response to our photography and experiences, while progressing through the journey, was also very encouraging.

My Expedition 13 crewmates, Pavel Vinogradov and Thomas Reiter, whose professionalism is unsurpassed, made the expedition as near to ideal as one might possibly imagine. That can also be said for the other eighteen space travelers I was privileged to work with on the International Space Station.

I found that organizing *The Work of His Hands* and putting the experience into words was difficult. I am greatly indebted to my friend Jay Flowers, who provided valuable comments and suggestions after a meticulous review of an early manuscript.

Finally, I am grateful to the team from Concordia Publishing House for encouraging me to take on the task, offering me the opportunity, and dedicating their attention to detail in the editing and publishing process.

Soli Deo Gloria

Introduction

This cause of exploration and discovery is not an option we choose; it is a desire written in the human heart. We are that part of creation which seeks to understand all creation. —President George W. Bush, eulogy for the space shuttle *Columbia* crew, February 4, 2003

The history of humankind is a history of exploration and discovery. Think about the voyages of Christopher Columbus, Ferdinand Magellan, and James Cook; the expeditions of Marco Polo, Lewis and Clark, Alexander von Humboldt, and Ernest Shackleton; and the *Apollo* moon missions. There is something in the human heart that seeks to understand the world around us, to explore uncharted territory, to know why things work the way they do, and to understand their interaction and interdependencies. This seeking responds to God's commission in the first chapter of Genesis to "fill the earth and *subdue* it" (v. 28). The curiosity of the unknown and how it relates to us extends toward and beyond the microscopic as well as toward the galactic.

In the case of space exploration, some of our curiosity can be satisfied through the means of unmanned probes, remote sensors, telescopes, and robots. But, ultimately, we have to go there. We need to witness and experience being in space and observing it directly. We need to put our hands on it and bring it back. We need to have a firsthand account. We need to journey. We need the profound effect the journey has on us. That need is written on our hearts. It is part of our created nature.

We are created in the image of God, and we desire to know Him. And in knowing Him, we come to understand and know ourselves. Creation testifies to God's existence, proclaims His glory, and causes us

Creation testifies to God's existence, proclaims His glory.

to contemplate His personhood. The pursuit of understanding creation and knowing the Creator is unique to humans. A pet dog—as much as we may love him and his companionship—does not look at a majestic panorama with awe and wonder; he does not have the ability to comprehend the mystery behind it or put the wonder of the view into words. Neither does the dog have a curiosity to learn and understand. We do. That is a fundamental difference between the animals and us. And that characteristic is a testimony to the image of God implanted in our soul.

1

Space
Exploration

The International Space Station (ISS) has been described as the greatest technological undertaking in human history, and for good reason. Its level of technology and engineering intricacy is self-evident. Perhaps even more significant, the ISS consists of the assembly of major components from the Russian, Canadian, European, Japanese, and United States space agencies. Built in different countries, most of those components were not integrated, verified, and tested together before being launched. They had to be added to the structure and integrated in orbit. Since the launch of the first component in 1998, the assembly of the ISS has taken the better part of twelve years. In its development and implementation, technical challenges have often been eclipsed by bureaucratic, political, and diplomatic challenges as the international partnership not only negotiated the technical objectives but also navigated a landscape of ever-changing realities and assumptions. By the time assembly is complete, more than forty space shuttle flights and an equivalent number of Russian *Soyuz* and *Proton* launches, as well as the rotation of expeditionary crews to and from earth, will have been dedicated to the assembly and sustainment of the ISS.

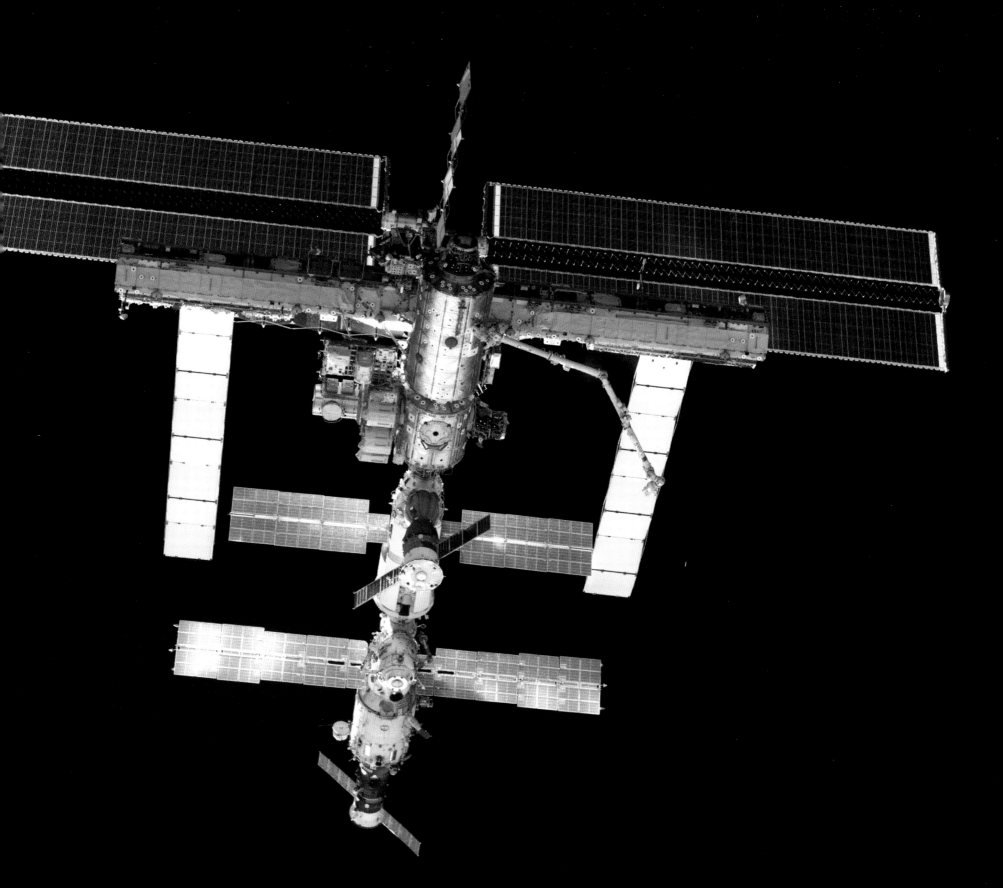

The first component of the ISS—*Zarya*—was launched on a Russian Proton rocket from the Baikonur Cosmodrome, Kazakhstan, in November 1998. Roughly two weeks later, the assembly began as part of space shuttle mission STS-88. The first ISS crew—Expedition 1—launched from Baikonur on a Russian Soyuz rocket about two years later in November 2000, and since then, a continual presence in space has been maintained on the ISS. After Expedition 1, expeditions rotated to the ISS on board the space shuttle up until the middle of Expedition 6—when the *Columbia* accident grounded the shuttle fleet in 2003. It was deemed necessary to continue the permanent manning of the ISS while the shuttle problems were resolved, and the Russian Soyuz became the sole means to rotate crews. Additionally, the loss of shuttle availability reduced the ability to supply the ISS. Therefore, the crew size was reduced from a crew of three to a crew of two to manage the logistical requirements. Expedition 7, and those through the first half of Expedition 13, had a crew of two—one American astronaut and one Russian

cosmonaut. With the return of the shuttle to operational status in July 2006, the crew size returned to three with the addition of a German astronaut. It is Expedition 13 that this book is about—a personal story told, in great part, through photography.

The ISS provides a unique and robust laboratory for science and research in a long-duration environment of weightlessness. Much has been accomplished already, and the future promises much more. But there is more to the ISS than a one-of-a-kind laboratory. It is not an end unto itself, but a means to an end. The ISS is only the current operational endeavor in human space exploration. It will help enable the vision for the future, sending humans back to the moon for the long term and, eventually, on to Mars and elsewhere. The ISS will provide the much needed experience in operating and sustaining a manned spacecraft over a long period of time—experience critical from the perspectives of both the flight crew and the ground crew as well as program management and integration. The international experience will likely apply to future programs as well. In those ways and more, the ISS will accomplish its purpose as a means in support of future exploration.

International Preparations and Means

Crew training and preparations for the members of Expedition 13 began late in the summer of 2002. At the time, the international partnership of the ISS was operating under a set of assumptions completely different from what eventually came to pass. The tragedy of the space shuttle *Columbia* and the loss of the STS-107 crew had not yet occurred. ISS crew rotations were all being conducted on the space shuttle. The Soyuz spacecraft, which has an orbital life limit of about 7 months, had always been used as an emergency escape vehicle for the ISS crew. Up until the *Columbia* accident, independent Russian crews would deliver each new Soyuz and spend a week or so at the ISS before returning to Earth in the soon-to-be-expired older Soyuz.

Everything changed on February 1, 2003. The *Columbia* tragedy forced a grounding of the shuttle fleet until the problems could be identified and corrected. The Russian partners filled the gap by using the Soyuz to rotate crews starting with the launch of Expedition 7 and the return of Expedition 6 to Earth. Without the space shuttle to resupply the ISS and continue the assembly, the crew size was reduced from three to two—one American astronaut and one Russian cosmonaut—and they were given the primary mission to maintain the ISS until the shuttle returned to flight status and assembly could resume. Expeditions—the period of time each crew remained on board the ISS—grew to a planned length of six months. Because of the additional Soyuz training required, as well as training in the Russian *Orlan* spacesuit that is used during space walks, the time required for training in Russia increased.

The central region of the Baikonur Cosmodrome as viewed from the ISS passing overhead. In view are the facilities used to ready the Soyuz rocket for launch as well as the launchpad.

As we completed our early training, most crew members served initially on a backup crew to a dedicated expedition. Those who trained as part of a backup crew would later rotate into being a prime crew. Early on in the training program, some of us spent two weeks in Montreal, Canada, becoming certified on the Space Station Robotic System. After that, the "routine" travel schedule consisted of alternating for four to eight weeks at a time between NASA's Johnson Space Center in Houston, Texas, and the Yuri Gagarin Cosmonaut Training Center in Star City, Russia. (Training for each dedicated expedition spans several years.) The final two months of training and preparation takes place in Star City; then, for the last two weeks prior to launch, the crew is transported to Baikonur, Kazakhstan, for launch preparations and the countdown to launch.

For many ISS expedition crew members, the most challenging part is learning the foreign language. All of the Russian cosmonauts study the English language. All other international partner astronauts know or learn English and all study Russian. Although challenging and often daunting, I found the Russian language training opened doors to the culture as well as a better understanding of my colleagues, and to many personal rewards that come with that understanding and the associated personal friendships.

Expedition 13 started at the Soyuz rocket launch site, which is located in the middle of what was previously a top-secret Soviet base built during the Cold War in the early years of the space race. The Baikonur Cosmodrome and the adjacent city of Baikonur were built in the isolated region of central Kazakhstan. It is a place rich in history, where all Russian manned space missions have been and continue to be launched from. The isolated community, built in the late 1950s and composed of a mixture of Russian and Kazakh people, has gone through several generations. The launchpad used for the Soyuz vehicles is the same launchpad where Yuri Gagarin—the first human in space—began his spaceflight on April 12, 1961.

The pre-launch period at Baikonur started about twelve days prior to our March 2006 launch. In the five weeks before traveling to Baikonur, we completed the battery of final certification examinations in Star City, conducted to formally certify our readiness for the flight. Following the certification, we participated in a series of traditional ceremonies, a rest period, and farewells. The final farewell at Star City was followed by a long flight to the city of Baikonur near the banks of the Syr Darya River on the central steppes of Kazakhstan, where final preparations for the Soyuz TMA-8 spacecraft and rocket were taking place.

2

Expedition 13

Rocket Preparations

Our arrival at Baikonur was our entrance into the pre-flight medical quarantine, and much of the time was lightly scheduled and restful, that is, until "rollout." The rollout of the rocket from the assembly building to the launchpad was a milestone that seemed to rapidly feed the building levels of anticipation and excitement, especially among the launch team and family and friends with whom I was able to visit. We crew members had to participate vicariously, however. By tradition, the backup crew goes to the rollout but the prime crew does not attend, so that morning was relatively quiet for us. My insight into the rollout experience had been gained six months previous, while serving on the backup crew for Expedition 12.

For every rollout of a Soyuz, the slow rail ride begins at sunrise two days before launch. It is observed by engineers, managers, and technicians, as well as dignitaries, guests, and family, in what are usually very cold and windy conditions. The entire process of rollout and raising the rocket to the vertical position on the launchpad is seemingly simple and impressively efficient, taking only a few hours. The rocket on the pad is

The Soyuz TMA-8 first-stage rocket booster is shown here, with its center engine and four strap-on boosters, during final preparations a few days before being delivered to the launchpad.

The third-stage rocket booster and Soyuz spacecraft being lowered into position for attachment to the first- and second-stage assembly. The Soyuz displays the flags of Brazil, the United States, and Russia, representing the countries of each member of the crew.

The Soyuz TMA-8 rocket is delivered on rail from the assembly building to the launchpad and erected two days prior to launch.

the last significant milestone leading up to launch day. It is from that point in the launch preparations that time seems to accelerate.

Launch Morning

For every Soyuz crew, the time in Kazakhstan is mostly spent in the crew quarters, what is referred to as the *Cosmonaut Hotel*. It is a modest but comfortable facility located at the outskirts of the city of Baikonur, about a 45-minute drive from the Soyuz assembly facilities and launchpad.

After spending the entire quarantine time in Kazakhstan on a normal day's schedule—with a wake-up at about 0700 and sleep starting at 2300—on the day before launch, we were scheduled with a sleep period starting at 1600 (4:00 p.m.) and a wake-up at 2230 (10:30 p.m.) that evening. That did not work well for obvious reasons. I spent the first couple of hours completing last-minute details and then laid awake for the rest of the evening time.

My wife, Anna-Marie, and I spent a couple of hours together just prior to the sleep period, reflecting on where Providence had put us and was taking us. Our visit was a special time. Having endured nearly four years of travel, training, and preparation, we were both ready to finally get the journey underway.

After wake-up, we underwent final medical checks, took what would be our last shower for six months, and ate a Russian-style breakfast. The mood was light and spirits were high. Since the launch was still about eight hours away, I actually ate a substantial amount. Had I followed the pattern of an earlier flight, I would have eaten very little so as to not have much in my stomach when arriving in weightlessness—the conservative approach. But the previous experience gained several years earlier suggested it was okay to go ahead and eat well.

The traditional door signing ceremony came after breakfast. Back at our rooms we gathered with several of the leaders, the flight surgeons, and our families for that traditional event that included a few words of Godspeed from the senior Russian officer present. Then it was down the stairs, out the door,

Soyuz TMA-8 on the pad.

and down the path to the bus. The sidewalk was lined with family, launch guests, trainers, staff, and photographers. I could hear familiar voices, but with the bright light of the cameras and the accelerated pace of things, it was difficult to see and acknowledge everybody in the crowd.

As soon as we were on the buses—one carrying the prime crew and one, the backup—it was off to the Cosmodrome to get the Russian *Sokol* ("falcon") suits donned and pressure checked. They are full-pressure space suits especially designed for use on the Soyuz spacecraft to protect the crew in case of a cabin depressurization.

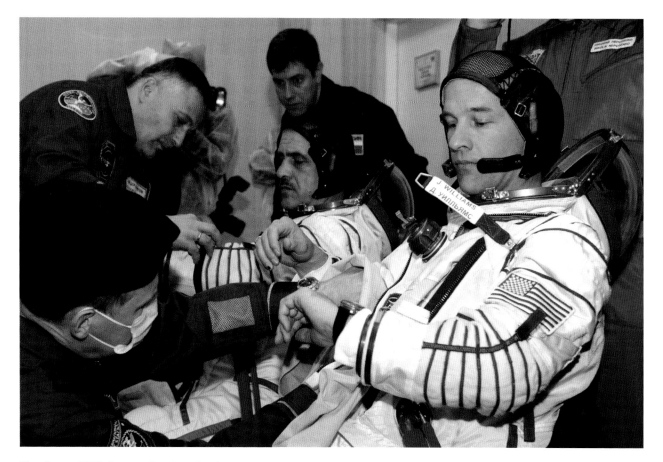

The Soyuz TMA-8 crew donning the Sokol space suits just prior to the ride to the launchpad. Pavel Vinogradov is in the center of the view and Jeff Williams is on the right.

The Soyuz TMA-8 on the launchpad.

Dear Lord, we have before us a most unique challenge and opportunity. We do not know what will be in store on this expedition as we fulfill the duties of our vocation. Lord, You have relinquished Your creation to us and gave us the commission to subdue Your creation. In it, You have given us all of the resources necessary to accomplish Your calling. You gave us the capacity for dreaming, for learning, for understanding, and the application of that understanding. May we use that capacity to fulfill the calling You gave us in this task. And Lord, while we are away, protect and comfort our families. Give them peace and the assurance of our safe return. And bring us to a safe and joyful reunion. Amen.

The traditional door signing, completed just prior to departing the Baikonur crew quarters for launch.

At the Launchpad

Arriving at the launchpad initially gave me the same feeling as the previous space shuttle experience. The hissing and venting of the rocket makes it obvious that it is fueled and ready to go. A big difference was the presence of many people just a few yards away from the base of the rocket—managers, technicians, media, and others calling us by name and wishing us a good flight. When you arrive at the pad for a shuttle launch, with the exception of the five people on the closeout crew who help you get strapped in, everybody is at least three miles away! We got off the crew bus and reported to Anatoly Perminov, the head of the Russian Space Agency (*Roscosmos*), along with other Russian senior leadership. Each crew member was walked to the pad elevator

From top to bottom: Jeff Williams, Marcos Pontes, and Pavel Vinogradov give their final wave from the base of the launchpad.

with someone on each side of us, holding our arms as we navigated our way in the awkward **Sokol** suits and carrying ventilation fans.

As we approached the rocket, I was struck by another strong impression quite different from the shuttle experience. Approaching the space shuttle *Atlantis* six years previous for STS-101, it felt like we were getting ready to go fly a flight and execute a quick mission. However, this time we were preparing to launch, get to orbit, and begin an expedition months long—the details of which were yet unknown. I was not even thinking about my return from orbit. It was too far in the future to be part of the impression.

Arriving at the base of a short ladder, we climbed a few steps above the ground and turned around to give the traditional wave, and then together with those attending us, crowded into a small elevator for the ride to the top and the ingress hatch.

Getting into our seats in the capsule—what we call *ingress*—was made slightly more difficult because of being crowded by the amount of cargo we were taking up to the ISS. We shared both the habitation module and the descent module, where our seats were located, with the cargo. These cramped quarters, filled by those things that would make life in space possible, brought home the realization that the spacecraft was the real thing.

To get into the left seat, I had to lower myself down into the center seat, lie down and partially close the hatch, slide carefully over to the left seat, and then get into what can best be described as a fetal position. Marcos Pontes and Pavel Vinogradov followed one at a time. Once seated, each of us slowly and deliberately connected ventilation and oxygen lines, communication and medical monitoring cables, and then secured the seat straps.

Now tied into our spacecraft, we spent the next two hours or so checking out the communication system, performing pressure checks of our space suits, and systematically preparing the rocket for launch.

Launch and Ascent

For the Soyuz, like most rockets, the dynamics of liftoff actually begin several seconds before as the engines go through the start-up sequence. This is when the vibrations started. Liftoff itself was a kick off the launchpad accompanied by a moderate shake. The acceleration or g-force was relatively low at first and gradually built up to about 4 g's (you feel four times your weight) at the two-minute point. Then a couple of significant events occurred, and if you are not prepared, they could be rather surprising. The first occurred with a moderate bang as the launch-abort system mounted on the nose of the rocket was jettisoned. A few seconds later, the first-stage strap-on booster rockets were jettisoned, resulting in an immediate drop in g-load from 4 to about 1 g. The shaking and vibration continued at a reduced magnitude as the rocket's main engine continued into second-stage. At a little over two and one-half minutes into the flight, the shroud around the spacecraft was jettisoned with a large "explosion" of pyrotechnics. Because of our launch time of day, there was sudden brightness in the cockpit as sunlight streamed in through the newly exposed windows. The transition to the third stage was even more dynamic because of a split second of weightlessness between the second stage shutting down and the third-stage rocket igniting. Our total ascent lasted just under nine minutes. At that point, the engines shut down and we became weightless. Traveling in Earth orbit at 17,500 miles per hour, we were on our way to the Space Station.

Orbit Checks and Maneuvers

The view from orbit is terrific, of course, but after launch there was not much time to enjoy it—at least for a few hours. As soon as orbit was achieved, pressure checks were required to insure our spacecraft was not leaking out our breathing air or oxygen reserves. Additionally, we checked out the flight-control system to make sure that orbital maneuvers, rendezvous, and docking with the ISS could be successfully accomplished.

While we conducted our procedures in orbit, the ground-control team tracked our orbit to determine the exact maneuvers required for rendezvous. The flight plan was adjusted over radio calls each time the spacecraft flew over Russia. Perhaps the most challenging part of the whole flight was keeping up with all the numbers called up during those communication passes. Since the passes were short in duration and a lot of critical information was required to be communicated—and all in Russian—it took intense concentration to understand and write down the data.

Not until several hours after launch were we able to get out of the seats, stretch out, and enter the habitation module for a short break. Then, after yet another orbital maneuver, we were finally able to take a long break and get some much needed rest.

Although small, the Soyuz spacecraft has all the essentials for living comfortably. Once established on orbit, we were able to get out of our **Sokol** suits and into regular clothing—at least until the final rendezvous. Plenty of water and food were on board, though it had to be eaten at ambient temperatures because there was no way to heat it. We even discovered some fresh apples and oranges, which were a special surprise.

Everybody had a sleeping bag, though I only used mine on a couple of brief occasions during the 48-hour Soyuz flight, and then only when getting a little chilly.

The Soyuz has three windows, and we used them a lot during the free times. The window time gave me a great face tan from the reflected light off the Earth. When we were not actively flying the vehicle, we put it in a solar-oriented inertial spin; that is, spinning at about 3 degrees/second with the solar arrays pointed at the sun. That meant that the out-the-window view was a sweep of the earth every two minutes or so. It also produced some unique motion sensations. You could actual lie down on the upper hatch of the habitation module and be held there by the slight centrifugal force of the spin. It also meant that everything not tethered tended to float toward the top. I slept in the midst of that unique situation by tying a loop around my index finger and hanging by the thread. It was a very stable and comfortable position, and I rested well.

Arriving at the Outpost

The final phase of the flight to the ISS is called the rendezvous. Rendezvous started several hours before docking and more than 40 hours after launch. We got back in our Sokol suits as a precaution, in case the impact of docking caused a leak in the Soyuz. We performed several maneuvers to set us on a path that would intersect the ISS's orbit. For the entire rendezvous phase, we monitored the steadily decreasing closure rate and distance from the Station.

The Expedition 12 to Expedition 13 change of command. Left to right: Williams, McArthur, Pontes, Vinogradov, and Tokarev.

Although we trained a great deal for rendezvous failures and manual flying, the automatic system performed perfectly. We approached the ISS, flew around it to align with our docking port (timed to coincide with orbital sunrise), commanded the approach, and smoothly docked to what would be our orbital home for the next six months.

After a series of pressure-integrity checks and removing our suits, we were given the go from Moscow Mission Control to open the hatches. The crew on board the ISS was very happy to see us, not only because they wanted the company but also because we were the relief that would allow them to go home to be reunited with their families. In other words, our arrival was their ticket home.

Upon entering the ISS, we spent some time greeting Expedition 12 members U.S. Astronaut Bill McArthur and Russian Cosmonaut Valery Tokarev. We also conducted a brief live appearance with Mission Control and then began the process of settling in for the handover activities.

Handover and Getting Started

Pavel and I spent the handover week with Bill and Valery reviewing the entire Space Station in detail, seeing how things work, where things are stowed, and detailing the best practices to get the job done most efficiently. There is no substitute for experience, and the six months Bill and Valery had on orbit was apparent and very valuable to us.

After the traditional change-of-command ceremony between the two crews, we said our farewells and helped get Bill, Valery, and Marcos into their Soyuz, which was flown to the ISS six months earlier. It was time for their departure from the ISS and safe return to earth and their anxiously waiting families. We were now underway as Expedition 13—one American and one Russian—beginning our six-month journey of exploration and discovery in the orbital outpost.

Expedition 13 Underway

Our normal activities could be put in several main categories, not much different than daily life on Earth. For example, we ate three meals a day and had snacks or a coffee break now and then. We lived on a 24-hour day using Greenwich Mean Time and had about 8 hours scheduled for sleep every night. Sleep was normally 10:00 p.m. or so with wakeup at 6:00 a.m. In addition to the experiments and research activities, we exercised every day to sustain muscle mass and bone density for the return to Earth in September. Periodic cleaning and maintenance, of course, were required just like any home or office. Equipment repair was also a common activity. Conducting our routine activities required a lot of supplies, equipment, tools, and other consumables, all of which had to be stowed, organized, and available when needed.

Because of the tremendous number of items on board, it is impossible to remember where everything is. Yet it is vital that the flight crew, the flight controllers, and the planners on the ground know where everything is stored, or at least have access to the information. For that reason, every significant item has a bar code. We used bar-code readers integrated with a huge database to stow and later find things. The database was maintained at the Mission Controls (both in Houston and Moscow), and the planners used the database

View of Earth through the window of the *Zarya* module.

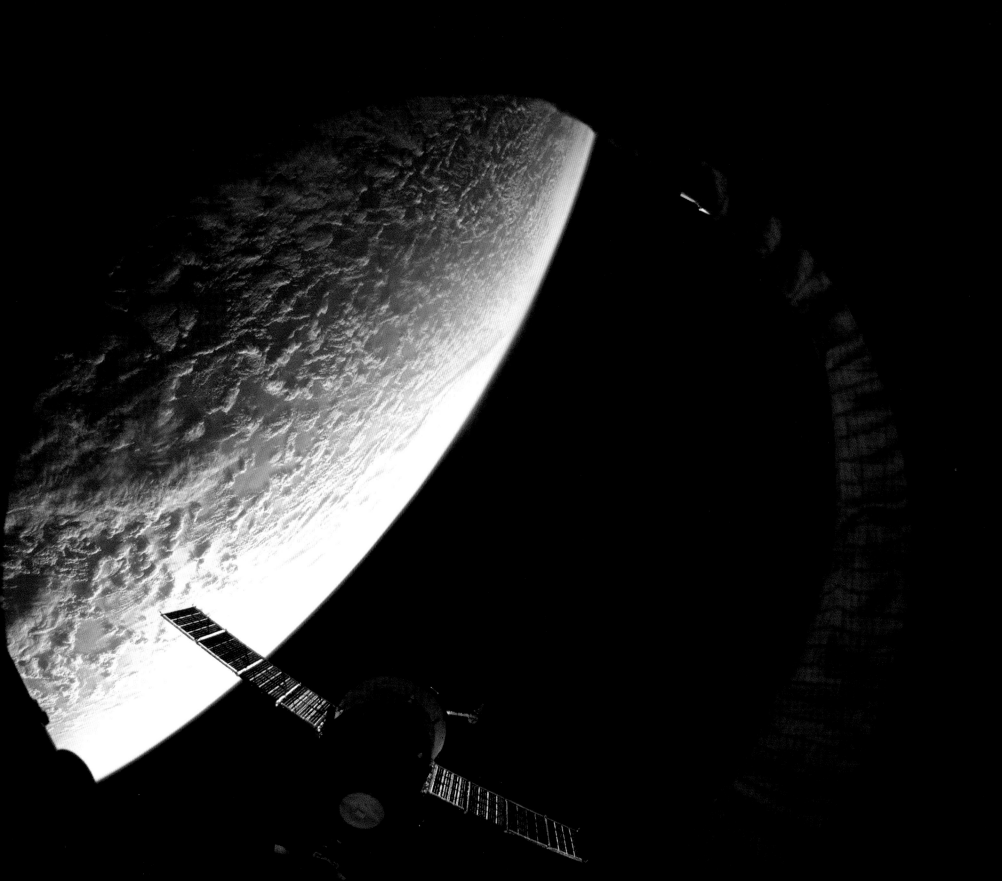

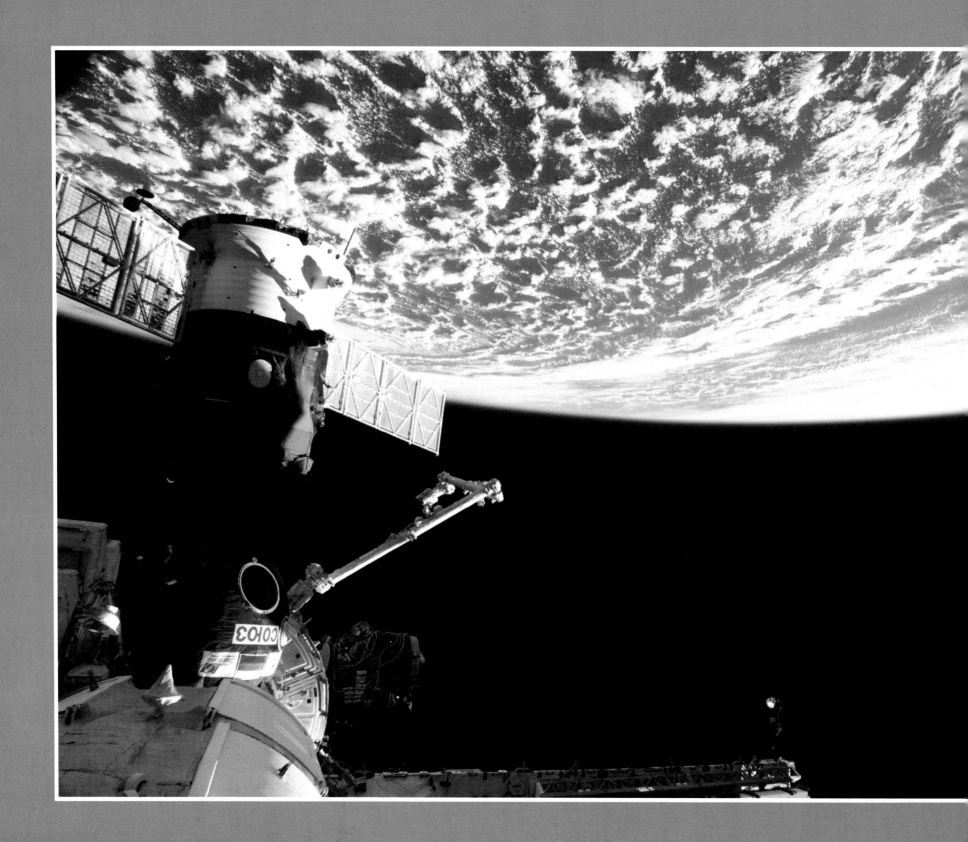

to prepare the procedures for our daily work. The necessary use of bar codes also meant there was a lot of extra time involved in working even routine things, such as deploying new food, clothing, or hygiene items, or moving things around for one reason or another. Of course, extra work was vital to keeping track of what was on the ISS, knowing where it was, understanding the resupply requirements, and building the cargo manifests for the Russian Progress supply vessels and the space shuttle flights. We had a great team on the ground keeping up on all of that and doing a great job of long-term planning.

People often ask what the typical day was like. But each day was different with unique challenges. Some maintenance was daily, some weekly or monthly, and some less frequent. The slate of experiments changed regularly. Equipment failures or other unexpected problems caused changes to the plan. Preparation for major milestones spread out over weeks or even months. And during certain periods, those major milestones, such as space walks or arriving spacecraft, dominated everything else.

Despite all the work, the required pace was that of a marathon, not a sprint. I learned I needed to maintain some sense of balance in daily routines. That meant rest, occasional reading, music, talking with family and friends and the like were absolutely necessary. Additionally, it was important to take advantage of the unique experience and impress the elements of that experience on the memory. That happened in part by photography and video recording. In a similar way, it was good to have activities that can be considered hobby or recreation. With all of that in mind, photography of the Earth below became an immediate favorite activity of mine.

3 Observing the Earth

The International Space Station provides a particularly good platform for Earth observation. The ISS is in an orbit inclined to the equator by 51.6 degrees. So, over time, the outpost passes over the entire Earth's surface between 51.6 degrees north latitude and 51.6 degrees south latitude. From the ISS, crews see well beyond those latitudes at oblique angles. That means that the vast majority of the Earth—except for the polar regions—can be seen and photographed from the ISS.

The ISS orbits the earth every 90 minutes or about 16 times per 24-hour period. Sixteen sunrises and sixteen sunsets can be seen during that time. With each orbit of the ISS, the Earth has rotated slightly more than 22 degrees, which means that a different portion of the Earth can be seen each time around. The physics of that relative motion combined with other impacts of orbital mechanics result in the entire Earth being visible at various sun angles, in day and night conditions. That, and the varying seasons in all corners of the globe over a period of months, provides a vast scope of viewing and photography opportunities.

Viewing the Earth from the ISS obviously provides an entirely new and wondrous perspective on the place we call home. During our time there, from late March through September 2006, we observed the northern hemisphere through its spring and summer seasons and the southern hemisphere through its fall and winter. Those observations included an endless array of subjects from seasonal weather patterns, to geological formations, to vegetation and agricultural cycles, to dynamic natural events, to civilization and human activity, and more. Natural history, human history, and cultural variations can also be seen as you study the detail from orbit. It is by such themes, interwoven with our major flight milestones, that the remainder of the book is organized.

But the Outer Fringe of His Works

Spaceflight definitely gave me a new perspective on the world around us and provided, in a very unique way, sort of a transcendent view of things above and beyond the immediate elements of life. For example, viewing the Earth from space brought a new significance to the truth of many familiar biblical texts.

There is a fascinating passage in the Old Testament Book of Job that I have marveled at for years and now has special significance to me. It speaks of God's greatness manifested in His creation. A normal response to viewing Earth from orbit is to be humbled and feel small and insignificant. Reading Job 26 invokes the same response. Any space traveler who has seen the Earth from orbit completely understands this sentence from Job:

"[God] stretches out the north over the void and hangs the earth on nothing." *Job 26:7*

When one views the Earth from orbit through the window of a spacecraft for the first time—and, perhaps, most every time—it is normal to be struck by the (obvious) reality that the Earth is a ball in the vastness of space. It is one thing to know that academically, quite another to view it. God really does suspend the Earth on nothing! Earth is a marvelously beautiful planet—the blue planet—orbiting the brilliant Sun in the middle of a vast universe populated by an amazing star field. The beauty of the colors, patterns, and variations on the Earth and in its atmosphere exceed the best of art. The horizon is wrapped by an incredibly thin and active atmosphere—an atmosphere we now know protects the planet and sustains life. Our home planet is a unique place in the observable universe. Viewing the Earth while being inside a spacecraft with all of the systems required to sustain our lives, one realizes that Earth, itself, is a spacecraft, traveling through space and designed with an intricate and robust life-support system. Observation and study over history has made obvious the significance of the atmosphere, the inclination to the sun, the water cycle, the magnetic field, weather, and the makeup of the earth in the sustainment of life, and all of that directly reflects the marvelous wisdom of the Creator.

Job goes on by saying, "[God] binds up the waters in His thick clouds, and the cloud is not split open under them" (26:8), a wonderful description of the most prominent and obvious element on the surface of the Earth. Cloud variations and formations are endless. The rapidly changing sun angles at orbital velocity and the seasonal changes experienced during a long-duration expedition increase that variety by an order of magnitude.

A later verse in Job gives an accurate description of what we call the terminator—the line that divides day and night on the surface of the planet. "[God] has inscribed a circle on the face of the waters at the boundary between light and darkness" (26:10). Orbiting the earth every 90 minutes, the ISS passes over the terminator twice in that time. The terminator cannot be seen on the ground, but becomes very obvious from orbit. How could the author of Job possibly describe the planet in that way several thousand years ago apart from supernatural inspiration?

Above: Along the terminator, long shadows produced by high-altitude thunderstorms illuminated by a low sun angle are cast across the lower cloud layers.

Left: A view of the Earth's horizon along with the ISS solar panels.

Those verses in Job 26 provide an elegantly brief but accurate description of the planet we call home. But Job does not stop there. After his fascinating and beautiful description of the Earth in such an economy of words, he comes to the conclusion and declares that such beauty does not even begin to approach the fullness, majesty, and power of almighty God. "Behold, these are but the outskirts of His ways, and how small a whisper do we hear of Him!" (26:14). Creation, as observed and described by the biblical writer, points to a Creator, but, as amazing as it is, creation does not even begin to reveal who He is. No matter that the works of creation are so incredible. Those works are but on the *fringe*. Though the view shouts with beauty, it is but a *whisper*. Pondering that truth was humbling—more humbling than the view itself. We will come back to that thought, but first let us look at some examples of His works.

4

The Beauty and Order of the Planet

The diversity of the phenomena of nature is so great,
and the treasures hidden in the heavens so rich, precisely in order
that the human mind shall never be lacking in fresh nourishment.
—Johannes Kepler, Dedication, *Mysterium Cosmographicum*

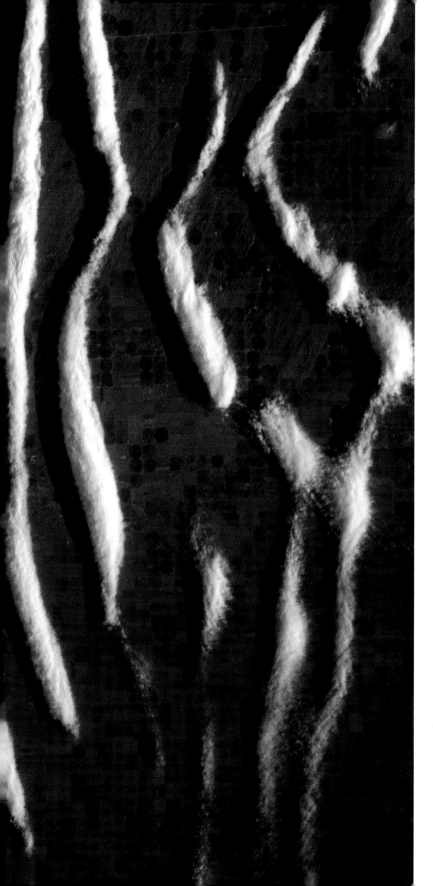

We love to behold beauty, even if we struggle to define what beauty is. It is no wonder that, throughout history, nature has inspired exploration as well as art, literature, and music of all types. The scenes of nature are frequently stunning in color, shape, harmony, and symmetry. There is also an undeniable order apparent in the observation of natural phenomena. Patterns and rhythms can be seen everywhere. They are often predictable and repeatable and reveal what we call the laws of nature and physics. Even in the midst of nature's apparent chaos, we observe order. Waves hit the shore at a predictable frequency. A stone thrown in the water produces expanding concentric waves that dissipate over time in a predictable way. Sand dunes form an orderly pattern. Observing that order in nature, along with the development of our ability to measure time, historically has led to hypothesizing and proving natural laws and the development of mathematics and physics. It has been because of the predictable order in the universe

Left: Rows of clouds display order in their pattern against the backdrop of midwestern agriculture in North America.

Far left: A low sun reflecting off the ocean with low-altitude cumulus and high-altitude cirrus clouds produces this mysterious scene.

Then God said, "Let Us make man in Our image, after Our likeness."
Genesis 1:26

Below left: Valleys of the Cascade Mountains in northern Washington filled with clouds.

Below: Low clouds, typical of the Pacific coast of North America, lap the coastline of Vancouver Island in British Columbia and fill the coastal valleys.

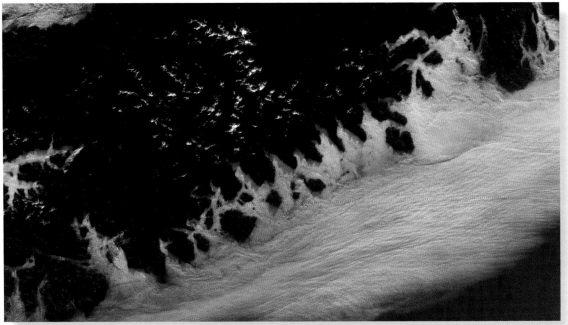

that we are able to develop the means to get to space in the first place and make further exploration and observation from that vantage point. A rocket is designed to fly a very precise trajectory with a very precise acceleration to achieve a very precise orbit in order to rendezvous very precisely with another spacecraft. The path of a spacecraft is highly predictable. Likewise, the entry trajectory and return to Earth are predictable. All of that is possible because of the order in nature.

That order is also apparent from viewing the earth from orbit. Seeing order in that observation produces a uniquely human response—an obvious awe and wonder at the earth's display of its

On Your wondrous works,
I will meditate.
Psalm 145:5b

Below: Various cloud patterns generated by weather systems, terrain, and high-altitude winds are evident in this view looking southwest over North America from the area of Newfoundland.

Below right: The layers of the atmosphere are displayed in characteristic colors and intensities at the moment of sunset.

unparalleled attributes. It is unique to human experience to have the ability and inclination to recognize and appreciate that which we consider beautiful. That is especially true in observing nature.

The observed character of creation testifies objectively to the Creator responsible for it.

And that exclusively human response testifies to the uniqueness of humans among creatures—uniqueness in abilities of rational thought, intellect, emotion, imagination, and self-consciousness, which all testify that humans bear the image of God.

Left column from top:

Gulf of California A complex interaction of wave sets and tidal currents displayed in sun glint are visible in this view. A low tide is causing an outflow of water, producing this peculiar interaction.

Lake Morari in Tibet sits at an elevation of nearly 15,000 feet above sea level on the Tibetan Plateau and is fed by melt water from surrounding glaciers. The prominent formation of sediment at the lake's outlet is called an "alluvial fan" and has effectively produced a dam and the resulting lake. The fan's apex was reportedly about 130 feet above the level of the lake at the time of this photograph.

Bulloo River in Queensland, Australia The floodplain of the Bulloo River and seasonal water levels form this very complex flowing pattern set against the backdrop of the dry, reddish terrain of this isolated region in the interior of Australia.

Below: The confluence of the Missouri and White rivers in South Dakota form this extraordinary downstream pattern of mixing waters of different colors. The White River flows through the Badlands National Monument in Western South Dakota and picks up the light colored silt that contrasts with the darker Missouri waters.

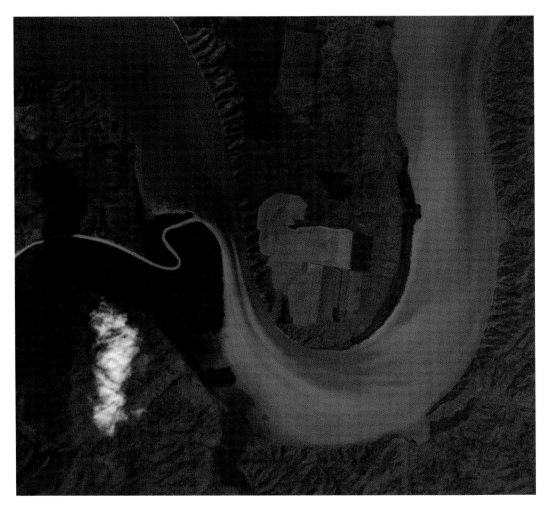

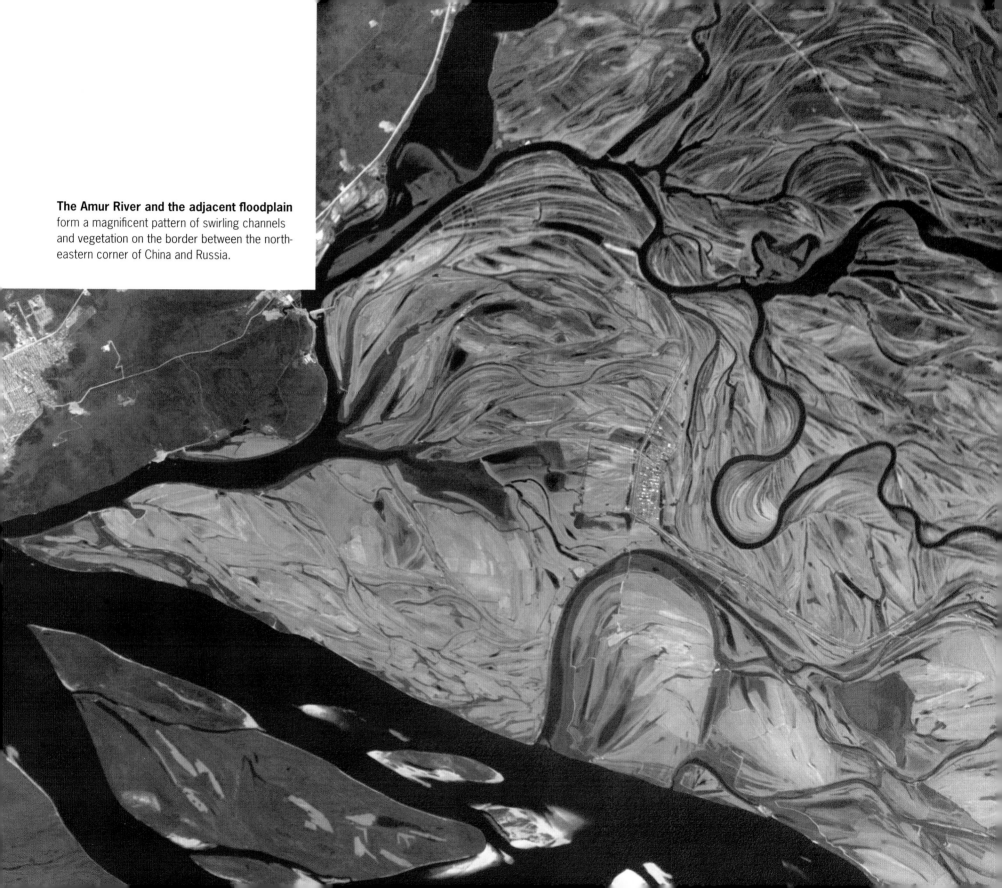

The Amur River and the adjacent floodplain form a magnificent pattern of swirling channels and vegetation on the border between the north-eastern corner of China and Russia.

The Betsiboka River delta in Madagascar is starkly beautiful in its flowing patterns and red color as it flows into the coastal plain and into the Indian Ocean. Off the southeast coast of Africa, Madagascar is known for its unique and varied plants and animals.

The Brahmaputra River flows out of the Himalayan Mountains and into the Assam Valley of northeastern India. The flat terrain that supports multiple channels and makes the river susceptible to catastrophic flooding from the upstream spring melt is apparent. The area is known for its wildlife, including rhinoceroses, tigers, elephants, and water buffalo.

Far right: The details of Niagara Falls are easily seen with the high contrast of the rapids and falls with the surrounding water and terrain.

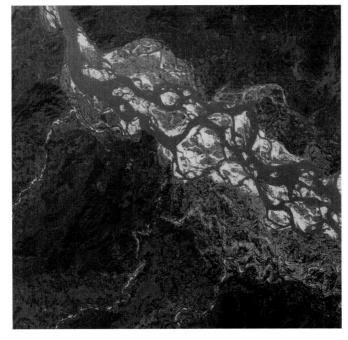

Lake Lanier, a reservoir just northeast of Atlanta, GA, is congested with recreational boaters, as evidenced by the many V-shaped wakes, on this beautiful day after Memorial Day.

'Tis wonderful how completely the earth is fertilized by currents of water running in all directions and constantly replenished by snow, rain, and dew.
—Martin Luther, *Table Talk*

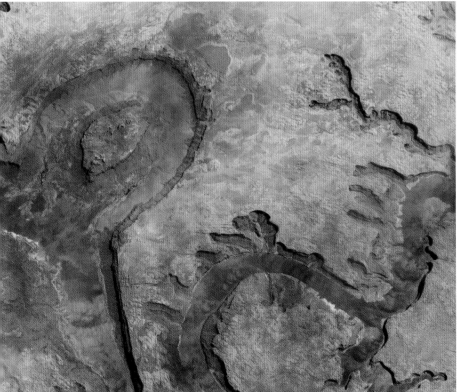

> Great is the power of God. He supports the whole world. . . . He has enough of everything for us. All the seas are our cellar; the forests are our hunting grounds; the earth, as our granary and pantry, is full of silver and gold and bears innumerable fruits. All things were created for our benefit.
>
> – Martin Luther, *What Luther Says*, § 4933

Above: Fan-shaped array of terrain in the center of western Colorado.

Top left corner: Lake Amadeus, a huge salt lake in the Northern Territories of Australia, appears as if it is the surface of another planet. About 90 miles long and up to 12 miles wide, it sometimes contains a few inches of water but is usually dry as seen here.

Left: Lake Powell, in southern Utah, exists because of the Glen Canyon Dam and fills a canyon nearly 190 miles long. The long narrow reservoir and surrounding terrain is beautiful from orbit. The horseshoe-shaped dry canyon adjacent to the river is known as the Rincon, an old meander prominent from orbit.

Right: This amazing large-scale swirling pattern of salt domes in the Kavir Desert of central Iran (32.7 N, 56.4 E), appears as though it was bent and folded in a fluidic state before solidifying.

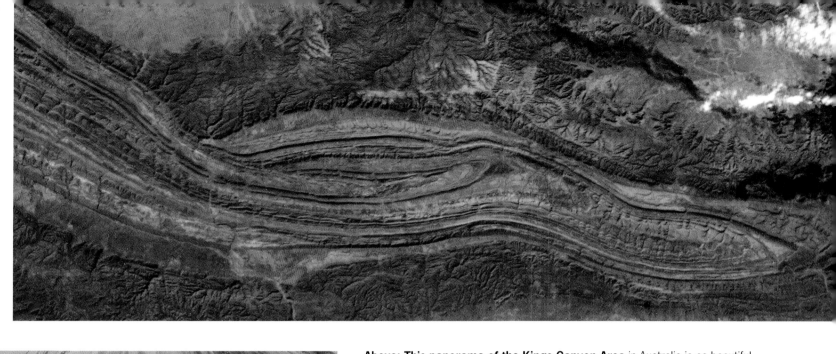

Above: This panorama of the Kings Canyon Area in Australia is as beautiful from orbit as it is reported to be on the ground. Note the small riverbed that appears to cut across the geological formations.

Below: The snow-covered top of the inactive volcano Kibo on Mount Kilimanjaro, Africa's highest point at 19,341 feet. Because of the elevation combined with its location near the equator, nearly every climate type on earth can be found on and near Kilimanjaro.

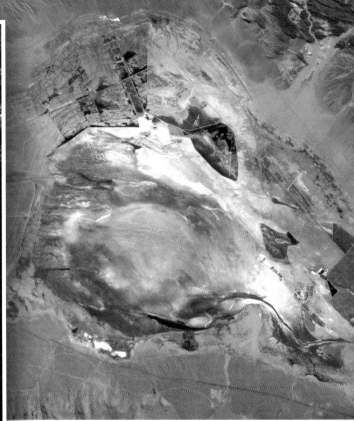

The Grand Tetons This south-looking oblique view of the Teton mountain range in northwest Wyoming clearly shows the 7,000 foot vertical rise above Jackson Lake. The Snake River—whose source is on the west side of the continental divide in Yellowstone National Park—flows to the south in this view before turning west and then north to flow into the Columbia River. The southwest corner of Yellowstone National Park is visible in the lower left corner.

Crater Lake, located in Oregon in the Cascade Mountains, is easily seen from orbit because of its characteristic deep blue water and distinctive round shape. As beautiful on its shore as from orbit, the lake has a surface elevation of 6,178 feet and is about five miles across. It is nearly 2,000 feet deep. Wizard Island, formed from a volcanic cinder cone and located near the western shore, is topped by its own volcanic crater (snow covered in the photo) that is about 500 feet in diameter.

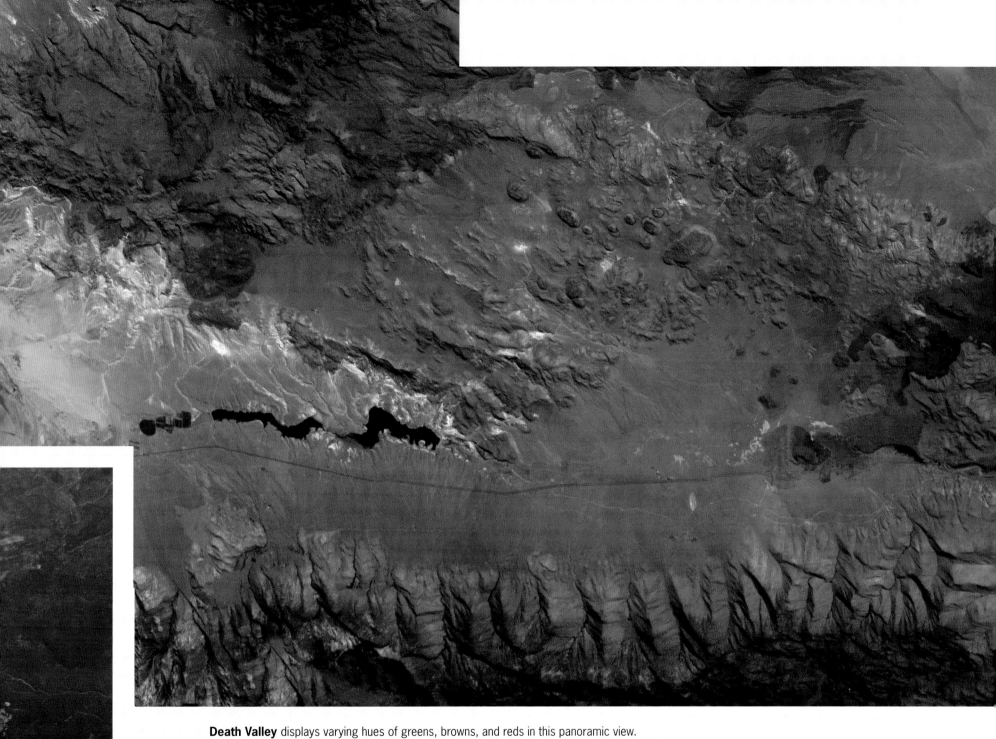

Death Valley displays varying hues of greens, browns, and reds in this panoramic view.
With the lowest point in the United States at 281 feet below sea level (located at Badwater, CA),
Death Valley often reaches summertime temperatures greater than 120 degrees Fahrenheit.

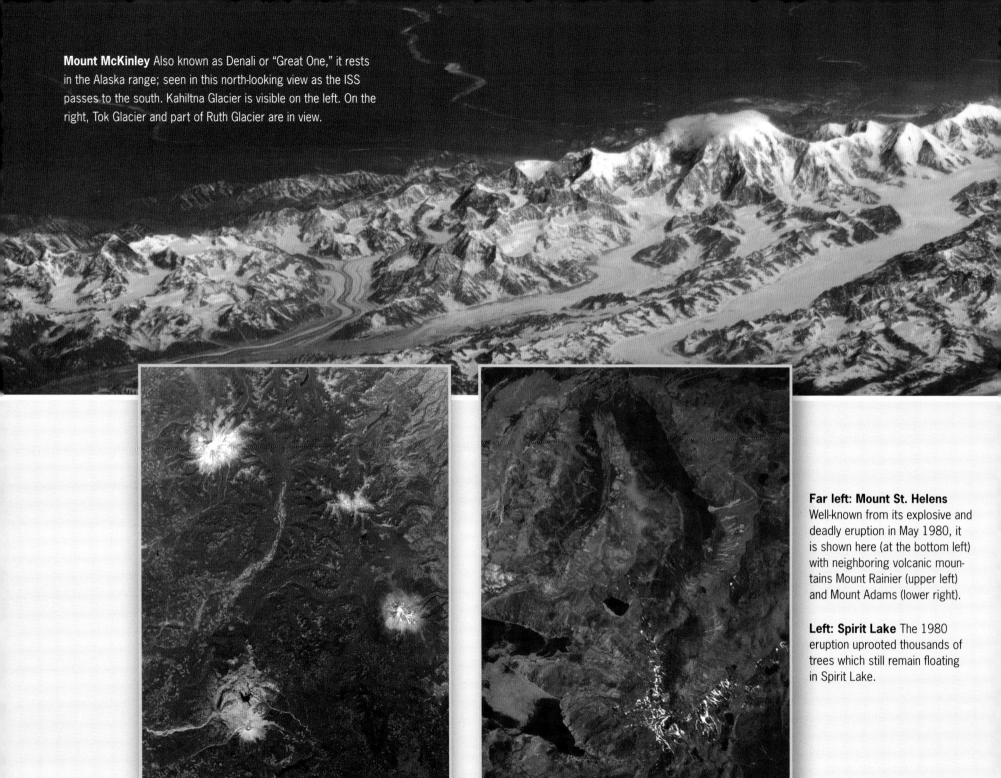

Mount McKinley Also known as Denali or "Great One," it rests in the Alaska range; seen in this north-looking view as the ISS passes to the south. Kahiltna Glacier is visible on the left. On the right, Tok Glacier and part of Ruth Glacier are in view.

Far left: Mount St. Helens Well-known from its explosive and deadly eruption in May 1980, it is shown here (at the bottom left) with neighboring volcanic mountains Mount Rainier (upper left) and Mount Adams (lower right).

Left: Spirit Lake The 1980 eruption uprooted thousands of trees which still remain floating in Spirit Lake.

Oblique close-up of Mount St. Helens Notice the steam rising from the summit. The mud flows that occurred during and subsequent to the 1980 eruption have blocked the previous outlet to Spirit Lake in the upper portion of the photograph. The North Fork Toutle River is visible in the foreground. Also visible surrounding the volcano are the distinctive patterns of forestry operations.

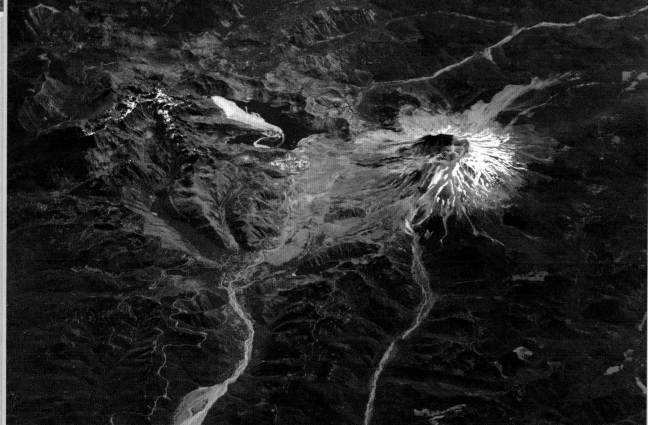

Northeast oblique view of the Swiss Alps Among the most prominent features are the Aletsch Glacier, the largest glacier in the range, and the Jungfrau, Moench, Eiger, and Wetterhorn peaks. Lake Brienz, also in Switzerland, is visible to the north of the range.

Above: Grand Canyon National Park evokes awe and wonder for visitors—including astronauts viewing it from space. The transcendent and humbling experience I had in the 1980s viewing the world-famous canyon in person came closest to the emotions experienced when viewing the planet from orbit. The South Rim is to the right; North Rim to the left.

Top right: Brukkaros Crater The only prominent relief in the vicinity, it is an extinct volcano rising about 2,000 feet above the plains in Namibia in southern Africa.

Right: Andes Mountains This panoramic oblique view of the high elevations shared by Argentina and Chile has the appearance of another planet. The desolate area has elevations greater than 12,000 feet.

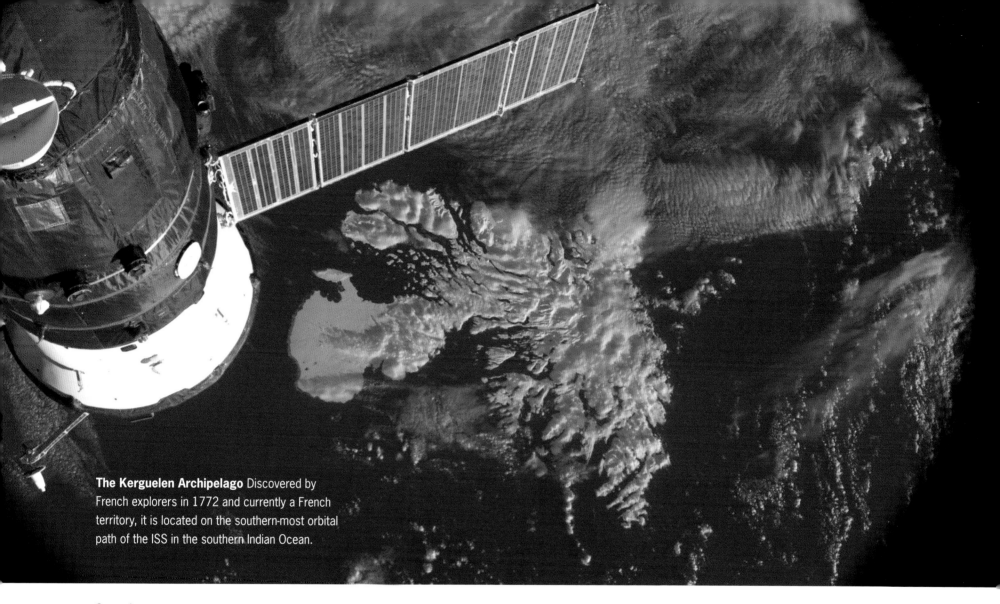

The Kerguelen Archipelago Discovered by French explorers in 1772 and currently a French territory, it is located on the southern-most orbital path of the ISS in the southern Indian Ocean.

Opposite page:

Top left: The coastline of the Russian Kamchatka Peninsula in early May before the spring thaw. This stretch is just southeast of the Mutnovsky Volcano, one of the most active in the region.

Bottom left: Clouds and glaciers meet on the top of these barren mountains located in the Himalayan Range—the highest on earth—not far from Mount Everest (28.9 N, 84.2 E) on the north slope crossing the border between Nepal and Tibet.

Top center: One of many glaciers in Patagonia during the middle of winter in the southern hemisphere.

Middle center: The ice fields of southern Patagonia include the Perito Moreno Glacier in the Los Glaciares National Park in Argentina, which is a popular tourist attraction because of a unique dynamic that occurs. The glacier advances up to 2 meters per day and periodically forms an ice dam, as seen in this photograph, across the Lago (Lake) Argentino. The lower part of the lake, known as "Brazo Rico," rises faster than the main portion and can reach a level nearly 100 feet higher. The hydrostatic pressure eventually causes the ice dam to fracture and collapse, producing a tremendous rush of water, and a spectacular show.

Bottom center: Unidentified ice field and glaciers in British Columbia, located at 50.8 N, 123.9 W.

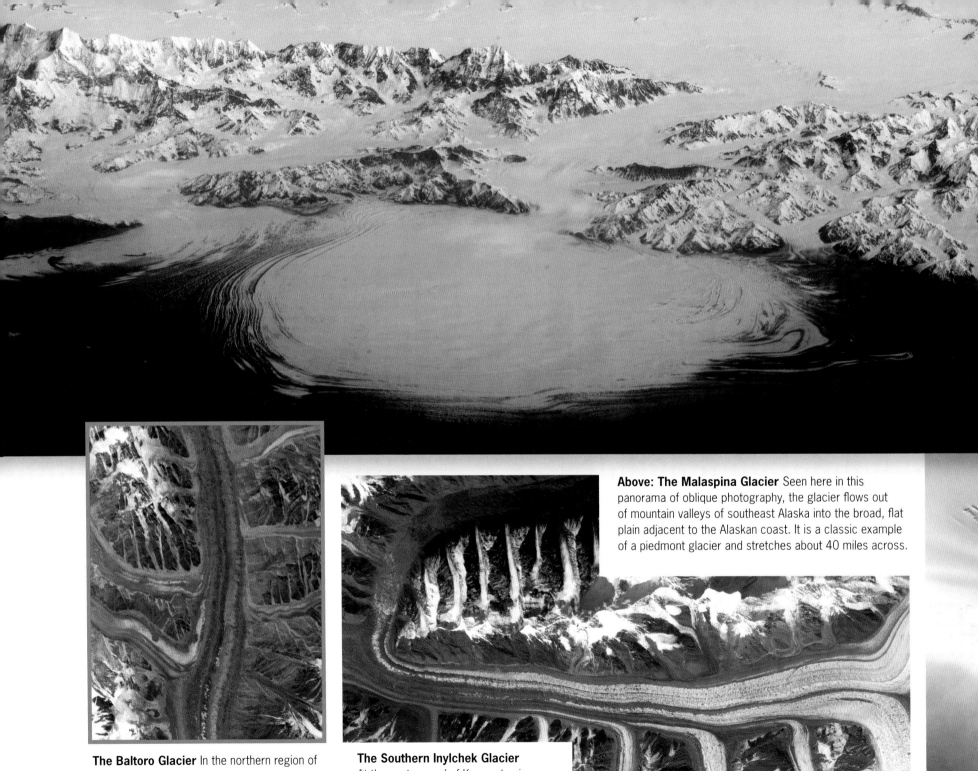

Above: The Malaspina Glacier Seen here in this panorama of oblique photography, the glacier flows out of mountain valleys of southeast Alaska into the broad, flat plain adjacent to the Alaskan coast. It is a classic example of a piedmont glacier and stretches about 40 miles across.

The Baltoro Glacier In the northern region of Pakistan, this glacier is one of the longest outside the polar regions. In view is the confluence of the Baltoro and Godwin-Austen Glaciers—known as Concordia, it was named by European explorers after a similar confluence in the Alps.

The Southern Inylchek Glacier At the eastern end of Kyrgyzstan in central Asia, it is among the largest in the region with many branches combining to form longitudinal stripes of moraines.

The large Argentinean ice cap in the Patagonia region of the Andes Range feeds several dozen major glaciers. Here, just north of the Perito Moreno Glacier, Spegazzini Glacier also flows into Lake Argentino.

Christchurch, New Zealand, visible here in the 250,000th earth observation photograph taken from ISS.

Southern Florida The Florida Keys and surrounding coral reefs are seen in this wide-angle view.

70

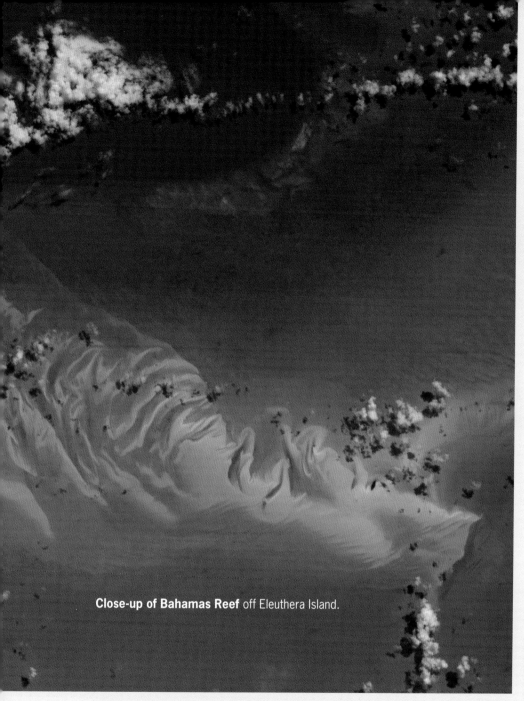

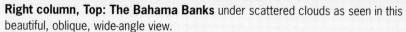

Close-up of Bahamas Reef off Eleuthera Island.

Right column, Top: The Bahama Banks under scattered clouds as seen in this beautiful, oblique, wide-angle view.

Middle: Cuba, under scattered clouds and adjacent coral reefs, passes under the ISS in this view out a window in the *Zarya* module. In view is a Progress supply ship docked to the Russian *Piers* docking compartment.

Bottom: The Bahamas, surrounded by the spectacular Bahama Banks off the coast of Florida, displaying a beautiful array of turquoise hues. The shallow-water Banks are formed predominately of limestone. The array of color is a result of steep changes in water depth, the darker hues being deeper water.

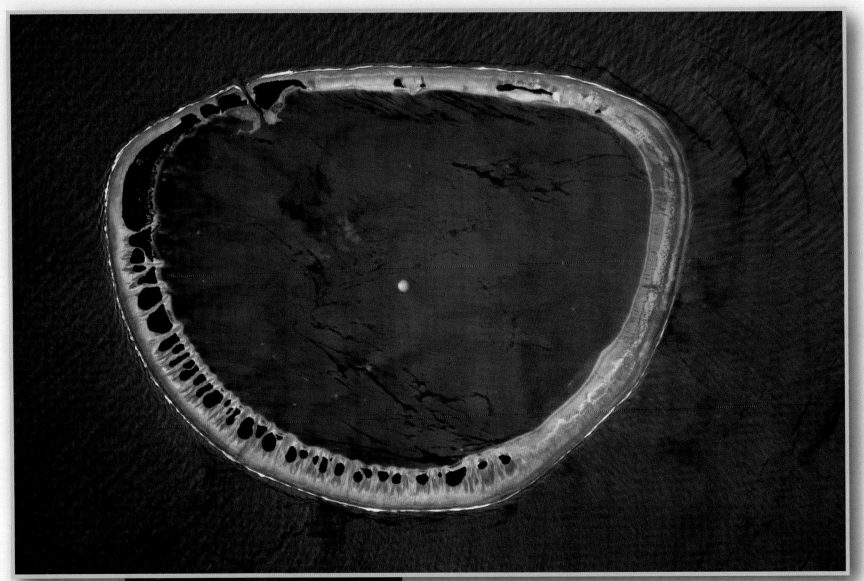

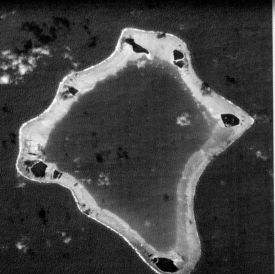

Nukuoro Atoll (above) is located less than 4 degrees above the equator northeast of New Guinea in the western Pacific Ocean. Nukuoro is one of the Caroline Islands belonging to the Federated States of Micronesia. The island has a diameter of about 4 miles and a population of about 900. The ring of coral surrounds a lagoon and supports vegetation distributed over half of the ring. Note also the coral heads visible in the lagoon as well as the detailed structure of the surrounding wave patterns.

Palmerston Island An atoll located in the Cook Islands, it was first discovered by explorer James Cook in 1774. In 1863, Englishman William Marsters settled on the atoll with multiple Polynesian wives. Today, the island has about 50 inhabitants, many the descendants of Marsters.

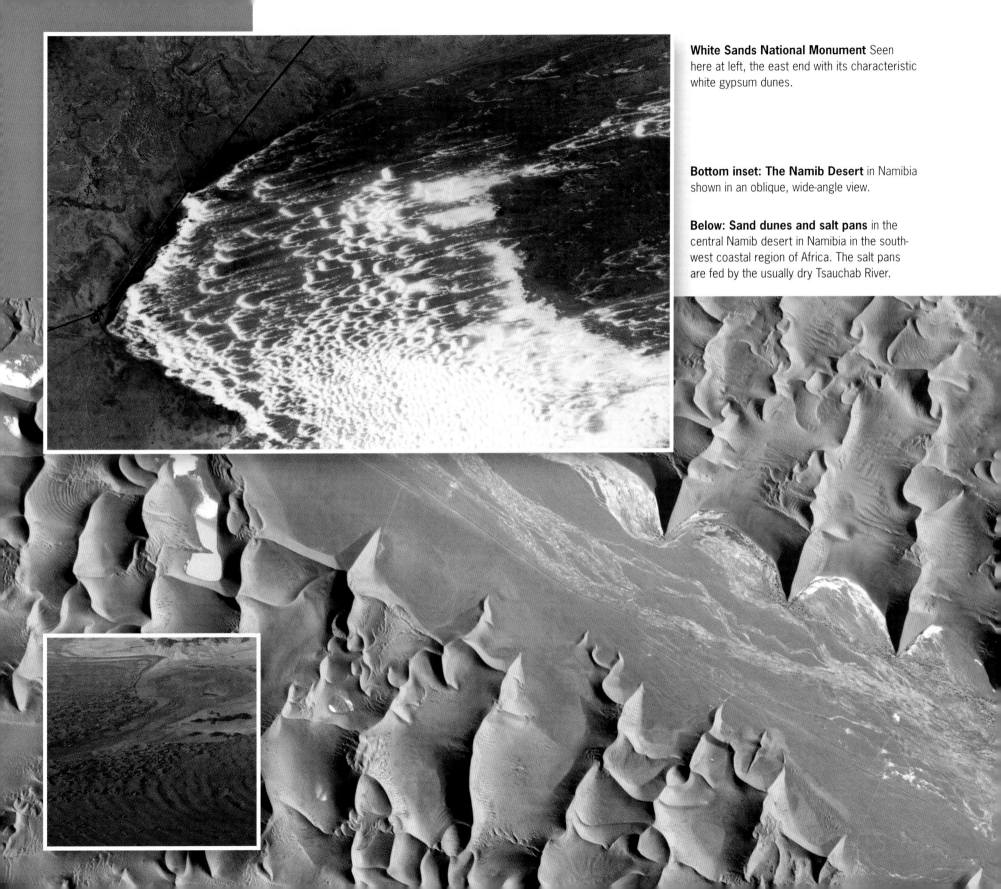

White Sands National Monument Seen here at left, the east end with its characteristic white gypsum dunes.

Bottom inset: The Namib Desert in Namibia shown in an oblique, wide-angle view.

Below: Sand dunes and salt pans in the central Namib desert in Namibia in the southwest coastal region of Africa. The salt pans are fed by the usually dry Tsauchab River.

The Richat Structure Known to astronauts as the African bull's-eye, it is a prominent feature of concentric rings with a diameter of nearly 30 miles. While it looks like an impact crater, it is thought to be merely uplifted layers of a geologic dome laid bare by wind erosion. The landmark is found in central Mauritania in northwest Africa.

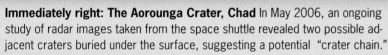

Western Mongolia This oblique view of a peculiar network of sand dunes wrapping around and between Har ("Black") and Baga Lakes and adjacent mountainous terrain. The area is known for its large variety of migratory birds and is becoming a popular remote ecotourist destination.

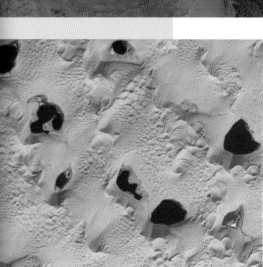

Immediately right: The Aorounga Crater, Chad In May 2006, an ongoing study of radar images taken from the space shuttle revealed two possible adjacent craters buried under the surface, suggesting a potential "crater chain."

Top right: Algerian dunes and mountains in the Kahal Tabelbala region.

Middle right: The Badain Jaran (Mongolian for "mysterious lakes") Desert Located in northern China's Inner Mongolia region, this desert features multiple spring-fed lakes nested among the very large mega-dunes. The sand field, situated in the larger Gobi Desert, has the highest dunes on earth, reaching heights of over 1,500 feet. It is thought that water from the lakes comes from the snowmelt off mountains hundreds of miles away, traveling through underground fractures.

Bottom right: The Issaouane Dune Sea, located in eastern Algeria. This beautiful display of large and smaller-scale sand dune patterns is apparently formed by prevailing winds. The structures reveal an intricate level of order in their formation and give incredible evidence of the order in nature.

5

Providential Sustenance in the Little Things

My hometown of Winter, Wisconsin and the small dairy farm I grew up on are difficult to capture while traveling at an orbital velocity of 17,500 m.p.h. My parents live there in the farmhouse my grandfather built after emigrating from Sweden early in the twentieth century and in which my mother was born. The surrounding forested terrain, lakes, and rivers constituted our playground as kids.

The Johnson Space Center and nearby Clear Lake.

The world is so empty if one thinks only of mountains, rivers and cities; but to know someone here and there who thinks and feels with us, and though distant, is close to us in spirit—this makes the earth for us an inhabited garden. —Johann Wolfgang von Goethe

Life on board the International Space Station is full of wonderful and interesting experiences but also presents the challenges of isolation and immersion. I can watch home go past at a deceptively short distance of about 200 miles below me. Yet the 200 miles is impassible in the conventional sense. The crew is far away from home: far away in calendar time, in environment, and in physics. It is not a trivial process to get back to the planet. The physics define a very large span between the state of orbital flight and the state of resting on the surface of the earth—a span necessarily crossed only via the unforgiving flight phase of entry. You cannot "just go home."

On the ISS, you are immersed in an environment that is continually watched and monitored from the outside. That, of course, comes with the territory and is necessary and largely positive, but it is still an immersion without break. Complete privacy or solitude is impossible.

Although weekends have a lighter work schedule than during the week, you can never really take a weekend break. Systems have to be monitored and maintained, and you have to stay vigilant, ready to respond to a malfunction or emergency immediately. You are also dedicated to a daily exercise protocol designed to keep muscles prepared for the return to earth, where, after the extended stay in weightlessness, the body will have to readapt to the seemingly harsh and unrelenting forces of gravity.

Another aspect of this total immersion is that of weightlessness. Everything floats—often away to unknown recesses—producing additional challenges for managing every item you work with. Weightlessness brings many unique experiences and is very interesting and entertaining, but after months of enjoyment,

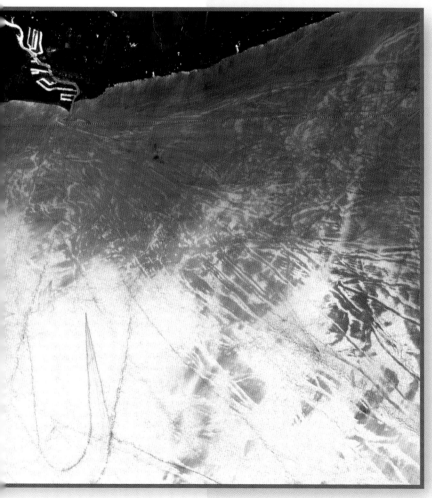

there comes a time when you look forward to the day when your food sits well behaved on a plate.

Finally, and perhaps most challenging, you are immersed in an environment of continuous noise—not loud or especially irritating—but noise nonetheless. The noise comes from the many fans used to circulate the air within the spacecraft to keep oxygen and carbon dioxide levels within healthy limits and to remove humidity. Besides family and close friends, among the things I would come to miss the most was quiet—complete silence.

All of those challenges are easily endured and overcome through seeing and appreciating what I call "provision in the little things." Recognizing the provision given from a gracious God produces and sustains a sense of gratitude even in the toughest days. Examples include cohesiveness among the crew, good relationships with the ground controllers, the ability to communicate with family and friends via e-mail and telephone, and care packages and fresh fruit sent on supply vehicles.

Another example—perhaps most significant—is to be able to share the experience vicariously with others and seeing their

Top: Labor Day boating on Smith Mountain Lake, Virginia Traditionally thought of as the last weekend of summer—a time to get in the last bit of summer recreation. On Labor Day, I again looked for active recreation taking place and found it here.

Bottom: Boat wakes in Lake Erie Using the glint of the sun reflecting on bodies of water, I captured a busy area of Lake Erie just offshore from Cleveland in this south-looking series of photos. Large cargo ships in and around the harbors of the Great Lakes are common, but the V-shaped maneuvering wakes of pleasure boats are not. Somehow, observing this traditional type of recreation provides a boost to your morale as you vicariously participate. Ironically, the boaters had no idea we were watching nor how much encouragement they were providing us.

enthusiastic and inspired response. And the gratitude, itself, has a reflexive quality to it and is a significant source of sustenance.

Unique provision and sustenance also comes through those special discoveries and observations made out the window. Following are some examples of sightings that, in a special way, sustained me during the long time on orbit.

Topping the list of special places to observe would be home: NASA's Johnson Space Center and the communities around it. It is not only our place of work but also our home and community. I made it a habit to report to family, friends, and the flight control team when we had a good pass over Houston. They also gave us a report when they were able to watch us as we flew over on other occasions. (When it is illuminated by the sun, the ISS is easily viewed from the ground on the dark side of the terminator.) Especially memorable were those rare occasions when I could call home while passing overhead.

On May 23, I was having "one of those days." Things were going fine, but I just seemed to be in a state of the blues. We were only eight weeks into the six-month stay and it already seemed like there was no end in sight. I was in the *Zarya* module with Pavel, about to head to the *Destiny* module for my next task.

Top: Boats racing in the Adriatic Just like family and friends vicariously participate in a spaceflight, the on-orbit crew can vicariously participate in sports and recreation happening on the surface. Here, a dozen boats—their wakes illumined by the sun glint—appear to be racing toward the coast of Italy in the Adriatic Sea.

Bottom: United States Military Academy at West Point There is an unmatched esprit de corps and loyalty among graduates of this historic institution on the Hudson River. As an alumnus, getting this shot was a special treat.

Tuesday, May 23, 2006

2355 hours: Absolutely amazing!! I just caught a brand-new eruption (at 2258 GMT) of a volcano in the Aleutian Island chain. The plume was fresh, and the lava was flowing fresh through the snow top.

Above: The eruption of Cleveland Volcano, Aleutian Islands, AK, on May 23, 2006.

Cleveland Volcano seen one orbit after the May 23 eruption.

Glancing out the window, it was obvious we were flying over the Aleutian Islands. *Zarya* has the best windows for photographing the Earth, so most cameras were routinely staged there for targets of opportunity. Grabbing the camera, as was my habit, I began snapping photos, first of one island, then the next, and the next. As I moved to one island, it occurred to me that something was unusual with the last one. Going back, the photo immediately to the left was in the viewfinder, and I quickly snapped a newly erupting volcano in the seconds before it and the plume were out of sight. The entire ash plume coming from Cleveland Volcano was in view, evidence that the eruption had just begun.

I reported the sighting to the Houston Mission Control Center (MCC) immediately, who then contacted the Alaska Volcano Observatory (AVO). MCC let us know they had placed the phone call, but that the folks in Alaska seemed a little skeptical of the report. Come to think of it, receiving a phone call from somebody claiming to be relaying a report from the ISS would be a little hard to swallow. So they sent up the contact information for AVO to me and I was able to call one of the scientists myself and—after convincing them it was not a prank—discuss the observation directly. It was a very unique opportunity for both them and us.

Pavel and I knew we had another good pass over the Aleutians 90 minutes later, so we were in the windows to take more shots of the active volcano. But as it came into view, we could see that the eruption was over and the cloud was detached and far downwind (see picture at the bottom of p. 80). Fresh lava in the snow top and extending all the way to the ocean was the only remaining visible evidence of the short, violent event.

It immediately occurred to me that being able to photograph the short eruption was a unique and special example of God's provision at a time when I needed it to bring me out of the slump. It did just that and carried me for weeks after. My wife, Anna-Marie, had known I was having a bad day and had prayed specifically for me in that regard. Her prayer was answered.

When you are isolated from friends and family, relationships we too often take for granted on earth, you desire to connect even from afar. One way you can indirectly connect is by observing human activity on the ground, especially if you can relate to that activity personally.

Noctilucent clouds over the North Polar region.

Memorial Day—the last Monday in May, a day on which Americans honor the fallen, those who have given the ultimate sacrifice for the defense of our freedoms—traditionally marks the beginning of summer and summer recreation for many in the United States. Boating is among the favorite recreational activities for the season, and Memorial Day is among the busiest boating days in many parts of the country. With that in mind, we had some great daytime passes over the U.S. on that Monday, and I watched specifically for recreational boats.

During mid- and late June, we observed a mysterious phenomenon occurring over the North Polar region after we passed into orbital night. These noctilucent clouds—also known as polar mesospheric clouds—brought a great deal of excitement to Pavel and me, as well as to the ground team, because the sighting was so rare and unusual, even for space travel. Noctilucent clouds, occasionally sighted from the ground (recorded sightings go back to the 1880s) are not well understood. They are located in the mesosphere—too high for aircraft and too low for spacecraft—and are thought to be made up of ice crystals. How those ice crystals get there is unknown.

I would maintain that . . . gratitude
is happiness doubled by wonder.

—G. K. Chesterton, *A Short History of England*

Sunsets and sunrises never fail to inspire. Viewed
through the layers of earth's atmosphere, producing
vivid hues of orange, yellow, and blue, they come and
go quickly due to the orbital velocity. The dynamics
make it challenging to capture them in photography.

The Russian *Progress 21* approaching the ISS on an automated approach.

Supplies and Notes from Home

Less than one month into our expedition, Pavel and I received our first shipment from Earth. On April 24, the Russian *Progress 21* cargo spacecraft successfully completed an automated rendezvous and docking with the ISS. That meant we were resupplied with essential equipment, food, and spare parts. Of course, the several thousand pounds of primary cargo took second priority to the fresh fruit and care packages from our families.

We first made a visual sighting of the *Progress* several kilometers away. Pavel and I were monitoring the spacecraft and its trajectory on the displays in coordination with the Moscow control center, prepared to take over manually if necessary. Since the automated rendezvous was proceeding without problem, I went to the starboard crew quarters window, found the spacecraft through the 800mm lens, and started taking photos. It continued to approach us from the starboard side, slightly forward and below until about 400 meters away, and then maneuvered to align with the docking port of the Station. At that point, Pavel monitored the approach at the command post and I went to the aft docking port window to monitor there and take some video.

It was amazing, not only to be in orbit traveling at 17,500 m.p.h., but also to have another spacecraft approach, ever so controlled, and dock with such precision at a relative speed of a few inches per second. During the final approach, we could easily see the plumes from the thruster firings guiding the spacecraft as they tightly controlled the final trajectory. In the end, the vehicle performed flawlessly and *Progress 21* docked exactly as planned.

After performing a series of pressure leak checks on the docking port between the two spacecraft, we opened the hatches and began preparations for unloading. The first thing was to remove the docking mechanism to make room in the hatchway for unloading. Then we installed a series of clamps to strengthen the docking interface and, finally, a ventilation duct to circulate the air into *Progress* and prevent carbon dioxide buildup while working in the cargo ship.

The first and immediate sensation after opening the hatch was the rich fragrance of the fruit, which included apples, oranges, grapefruit, lemons, and tomatoes. The personal packages included cards from family and friends, special food items sent by family, and other personal items such as photographs.

The primary cargo included several thousand pounds of spare parts, enough food for several months, consumable items used for hygiene and Station systems, clothing, equipment for enhancing operations, and some research equipment and experiments. It took several weeks to fully unload the supplies.

When *Progress 21* arrived, *Progress 20*—docked already for several weeks and emptied—became the place for trash. The *Progress* supply spacecraft is not designed to return to earth for a landing but, instead, to burn up in the atmosphere upon reentry. Trash disposal is obviously crucial. Because so much stuff is required to live and work in the orbital outpost, storage space is precious, and tightly controlled. Imagine the worst closet in your home. That's the environment the crew works in. So being able to load the *Progress* vehicles with trash was as important to us as the arrival of the fresh supplies—well, almost as important.

May 28

It is hard to believe we are approaching two months on orbit. Some days and weeks have flown by, some days have dragged on, but overall the time has gone by quickly. I continue to take it one day at a time, endeavoring to take in the whole of the experience and to bring it to you through words, photos, and video.

This week has been heavy in preparation for Thursday's space walk, when we both will venture outside for a little more than 6 hours. The several tasks will take us to both the Russian and U.S. segments of the ISS. We will prepare a vent for our oxygen production system, retrieve several experiments, and replace a broken external video camera assembly.

Preparing the Orlan spacesuit for upcoming space walk.

6

Russian-style Spacewalking

A Russian space walk outside the Station, or extra-vehicular activity (EVA), has about two weeks' worth of preparation. The tools, equipment, and replacement parts have to be gathered and prepared. Everything has to be tethered and packaged to support the detailed choreography of the excursion. The detailed plan, developed months in advance by the ground teams in both Moscow and Houston, has to be reviewed, then further developed and jointly reviewed again. Every detail must be covered, and all of the possible contingencies have to be addressed. The Russian Docking Compartment (which also serves as the airlock) must be prepared by removing all of the excess items stowed there, and the *Progress* hatch (docked to the end of the Docking Compartment) must be closed. Additionally, the Orlan spacesuits have to be prepared and sized, and the oxygen and cooling systems in the airlock must be readied. During the week leading up to the outing, the crew will conduct system checks, prepare additional equipment, and conduct a "dry run" of the airlock

Both pictures: Jeff Williams, wearing an Orlan with blue identifying stripes, installs a foot restraint on the mobile transporter in preparation for replacing a video camera.

operations up to the point of opening the hatch. Additionally, because Pavel and I were the sole occupants, just prior to our EVA we configured the ISS for unmanned operations and isolated the segments by closing the hatches. Typically, space walks are one of the highlights of an expedition. Such was the case for ours.

June 1 was the day of the Russian space walk for Pavel and me. Preparations conducted in the days prior went without surprises, and we were ready to venture outside. We ate a light breakfast before starting the day and then headed to the airlock to begin the detailed process to get outside. When suit up and depressurization were complete, we opened the outside hatch, and the obvious differences between training and the real thing began to appear.

June 5

You know a space walk went well when the highlight of the news afterward and the most often mentioned aspect was that our feet got a little cold.

We are settled back inside with the Station and airlock mostly back in a normal configuration. Pavel and I are very happy with how the outing went . . . all objectives accomplished successfully and safely. It feels good to have it behind us and now to look toward the next major event. I find that I mark the passing of time by major events.

With the opening of the hatch, the last bit of air molecules raced out into space, carrying all of the loose fine particles still adhering to the cloth lining of the airlock. For a few seconds, it looked like a blizzard in the hatchway. With the orientation of the hatch horizontal to the Earth below and away from the rest of the ISS, the view in front of us was only the black nothingness of space. Climbing out evoked an eerie feeling of entering into a vast emptiness until we were able to crawl completely outside and get turned around to face the ISS and the trail of handrails used to crawl around the outside of the ISS.

During an EVA, the crew and every free item of equipment or tool must be tethered 100 percent of the time. This is personally critical for the crew members for obvious reasons: anything that is allowed to drift away untethered is lost forever.

Crew members use what are known as safety tethers to secure themselves. One design type is used for Russian EVAs and another for U.S. EVAs. The U.S. design uses an 85-foot cable that reels out of a spool as the crew member translates across the Station to the workplace. Once tethered, you are free to move within the envelope of the 85 feet. The Russian design relies on two short tethers with closing hooks. The crew member moves hand-over-hand, moving one tether at a time as he navigates along the handholds.

Pavel and I were assigned tasks from the aft end all the way to the forward end of the Station. We installed a vent valve, cleared an obstruction to an antenna, retrieved a couple of experiments left outside on a previous EVA, and replaced a failed video camera—a camera that would be required for future robotic operations and the continued assembly of the ISS.

The successful space walk—*ISS Russian EVA 5*—lasted 6 hours and 31 minutes. It was Pavel's sixth and my second. All the objectives were met and, back inside the ISS, we were very pleased with the experience.

7 Visitors from Earth

On Independence Day, July 4, 2006, the space shuttle *Discovery* launched with her crew from pad 39B at Kennedy Space Center in Florida. The 115th shuttle flight and the 18th to the Space Station, STS-121 was underway after weather scrubs on July 1 and 2 were endured by both the entire team on the ground and us on the ISS awaiting their arrival.

STS-121 marked two major milestones in the history of space exploration. After three and a half years of investigation and redesign work, its voyage was the successful return to flight of the space shuttle after the *Columbia* tragedy. Additionally, to reduce the logistical challenges of supporting the ISS without the resupply capability of the shuttle, the Station's crew size had been reduced from three to two. STS-121 brought the crew size back to three and expanded the international participation, with the arrival of German astronaut Thomas Reiter representing the European Space Agency.

Like Soyuz, the shuttle takes about two days to intercept the orbit of the ISS. On docking day, we were able to see *Discovery* while it trailed the Station by several miles and as it rose above the backdrop of the Earth's atmosphere illuminated by the sun. It approached the Station from behind and paused at a point about 600 feet away, where the shuttle commander initiated a back flip so that Pavel and I could take detailed photography of the orbiter's thermal protection. That high-resolution photography was later sent to the ground for analysis to insure there was no damage that would jeopardize *Discovery*'s safe reentry into the atmosphere. After the flip was complete, the crew flew the shuttle to the front of the Station. It was an amazing moment to have the spacecraft flying outside the window in such close proximity and to know that we would soon be seeing our friends and welcoming them on board. The final approach was initiated, and docking was accomplished at the forward most point of the ISS. While both spacecraft were flying at 17,500 m.p.h., the docking process was a graceful dance executed with great precision. The contact of the two spacecraft was like when a refrigerator door swings shut and seals—and without the alignment provided by the hinges.

After *Discovery* and her crew successfully docked to the ISS on July 6, we opened the hatches to welcome everybody on board. The STS-121 crew consisted of veteran astronauts Steve Lindsey, Mark Kelly, Piers Sellers, and Thomas Reiter along with first-time flyers Mike Fossum, Stephanie Wilson, and Lisa Nowak. Having been isolated on the ISS for three months, we were thrilled to finally have long-anticipated visitors from Earth. The crew brought letters and gifts from home, and special treats such as fresh fruit. After greetings and a brief welcome, we got busy with the tasks on the very full flight plan.

The following day, we used the ISS robotic arm to remove the *Leonardo* logistics module—loaded with 7,400 lbs. of supplies, equipment, and ISS components—from the payload bay of *Discovery* and attached it to the *Unity* module. Once attached, we opened the hatches and began the long process of unloading the cargo and stowing each item on the ISS. After unloading *Leonardo* we transferred items and trash no longer needed on the ISS back into the logistics module for return to Earth.

The space shuttle *Discovery* flying in formation with the ISS.

Expedition 13, now expanded to an international crew of three, bids farewell to the crew of *Discovery*.

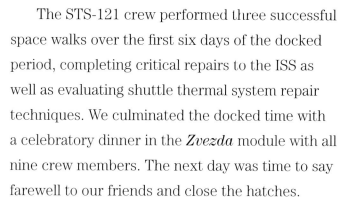

Combined crew photo in _Destiny_ module; from left to right and front to back: Thomas Reiter, Pavel Vinogradov, Jeff Williams, Stephanie Wilson, Steve Lindsey, Lisa Nowak, Piers Sellers, Mike Fossum, and Mark Kelly.

The STS-121 crew performed three successful space walks over the first six days of the docked period, completing critical repairs to the ISS as well as evaluating shuttle thermal system repair techniques. We culminated the docked time with a celebratory dinner in the _Zvezda_ module with all nine crew members. The next day was time to say farewell to our friends and close the hatches.

Leaving Thomas Reiter on board—now a member of Expedition 13—and with the STS-121 mission objectives complete, _Discovery_ and her crew undocked from the ISS on July 15 and landed safely at Kennedy Space Center on July 17.

With the shuttle back in service, ISS assembly could resume. We would likely be able to host another shuttle crew before our stay was complete. Additionally, we were now a crew of three—a Russian, a German, and an American serving together as one crew. The International Space Station was even more international.

8 Human Presence

Chicago, Illinois.

He is God; He who fashioned and made the earth,
He founded it; He did not create it to be empty,
but formed it to be inhabited. Isaiah 45:18 NIV

Houston, Texas.

Part of New York City and nearby Jersey City. Lower Manhattan and Central Park are easily identified and an abundance of ship traffic can be seen in the Upper Bay and Hudson and East rivers.

Many themes of human existence can be pondered by observing and studying the Earth's surface over time. While most of those themes are well-known to us from life on earth, through education, and media sources, they take on a renewed and somewhat philosophical significance with a stay on orbit.

It takes but a glance at the earth below to be reminded—with new significance—that it is truly habitable and inhabited. Weather patterns and oceans reveal components of the water cycle, critical to sustaining life. Variations of greens and browns in the landmasses and visible displays of land use show the fruit of the earth in vegetation and the production of food. Small plumes from factories are a reminder of the products we use and often take for granted—made from the raw materials of Earth. Cities, road systems, railways, aviation activities, ports and waterways reveal the commerce and industries of varying and interacting civilizations. Patterns and forms of human activity reveal cultural and historic details.

Following are some examples of observing the Earth from ISS and seeing it inhabited.

Munich, Germany.

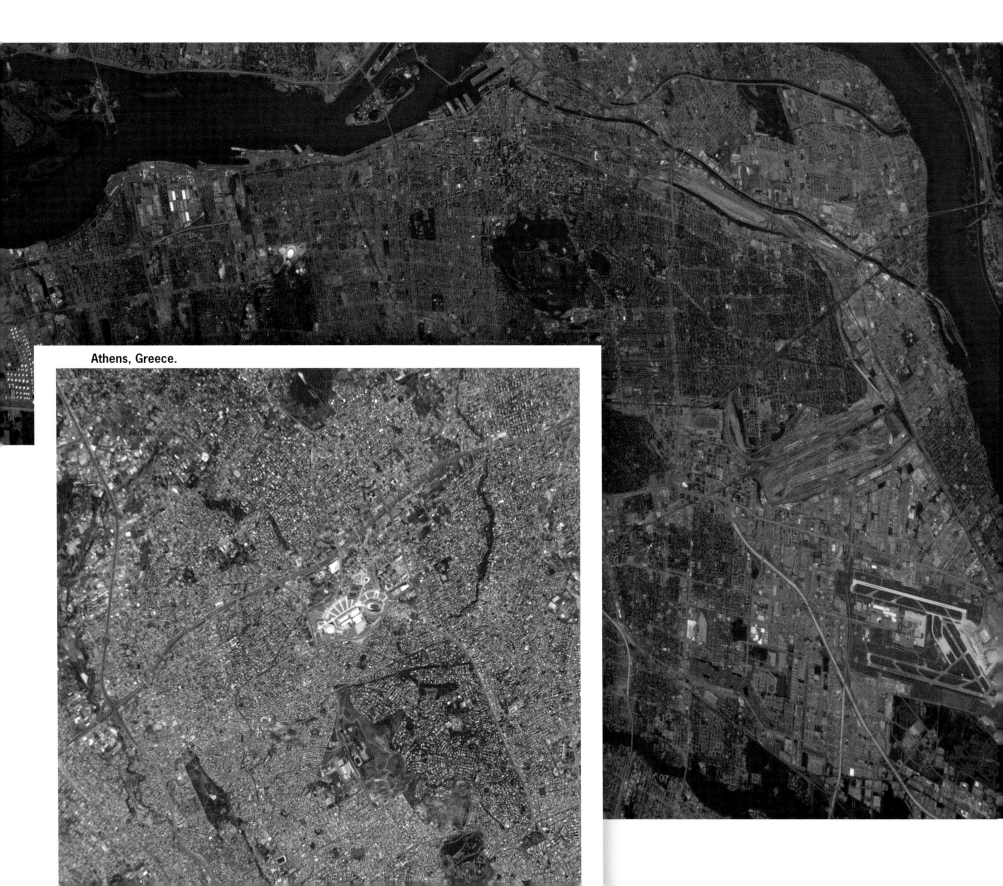

Athens, Greece.

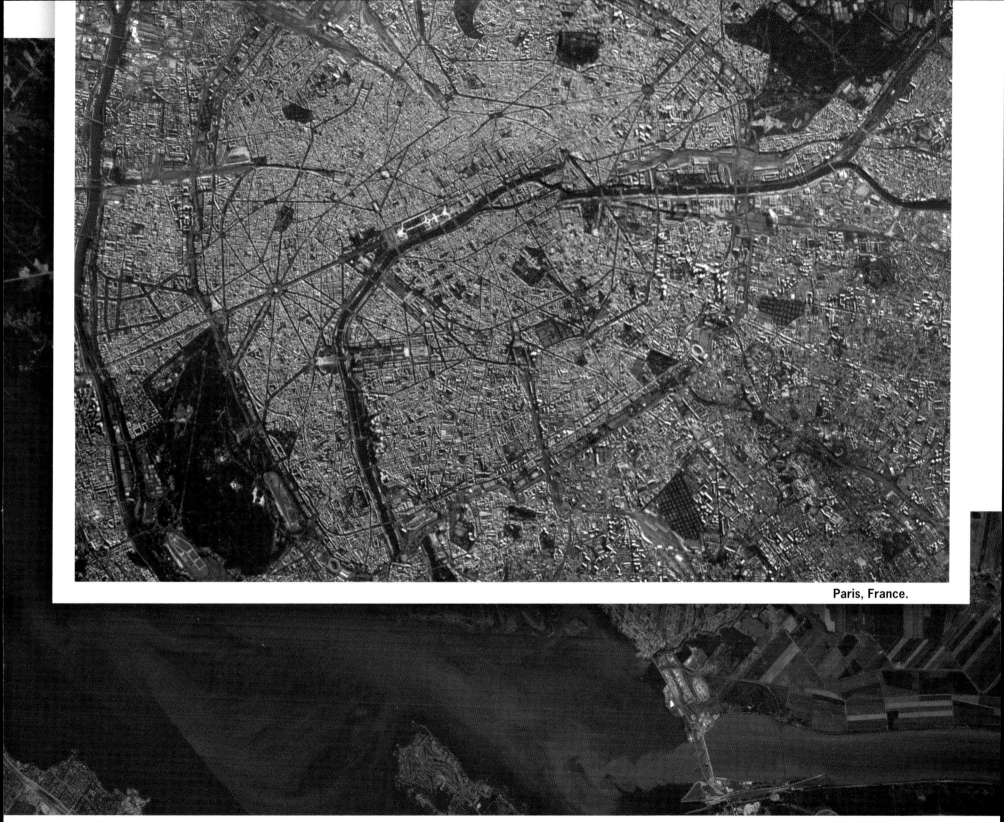

Paris, France.

Montreal, Canada.

Kuwait City, Kuwait.

Tehran, Iran.

Beruit, Lebanon

The Golden Gate Bridge—the famous landmark stretching between San Francisco, California, and the rugged terrain south of Sausalito—is central in this view. The distinctive orange vermilion towers of the bridge, mid-morning shadows, and wakes from ship traffic are easily distinguished. Details of the Presidio of San Francisco—an Army Post until 1994 and now a park operated by the National Park Service—south of the bridge are clearly seen, as well as the Fisherman's Wharf area and nearby Alcatraz Island.

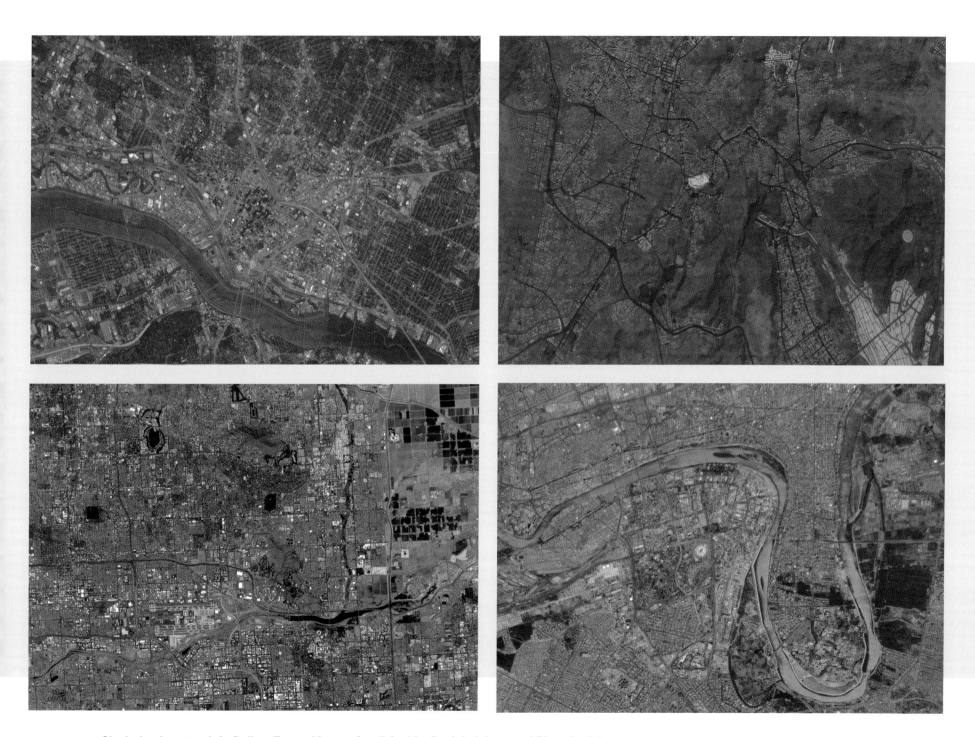

Clockwise from top left: Dallas, Texas; Mecca, Saudi Arabia; Baghdad, Iraq; and Phoenix, Arizona.

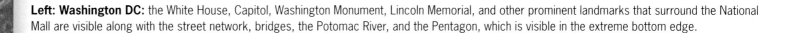

Left: Washington DC: the White House, Capitol, Washington Monument, Lincoln Memorial, and other prominent landmarks that surround the National Mall are visible along with the street network, bridges, the Potomac River, and the Pentagon, which is visible in the extreme bottom edge.

Below: Quebec City, Canada.

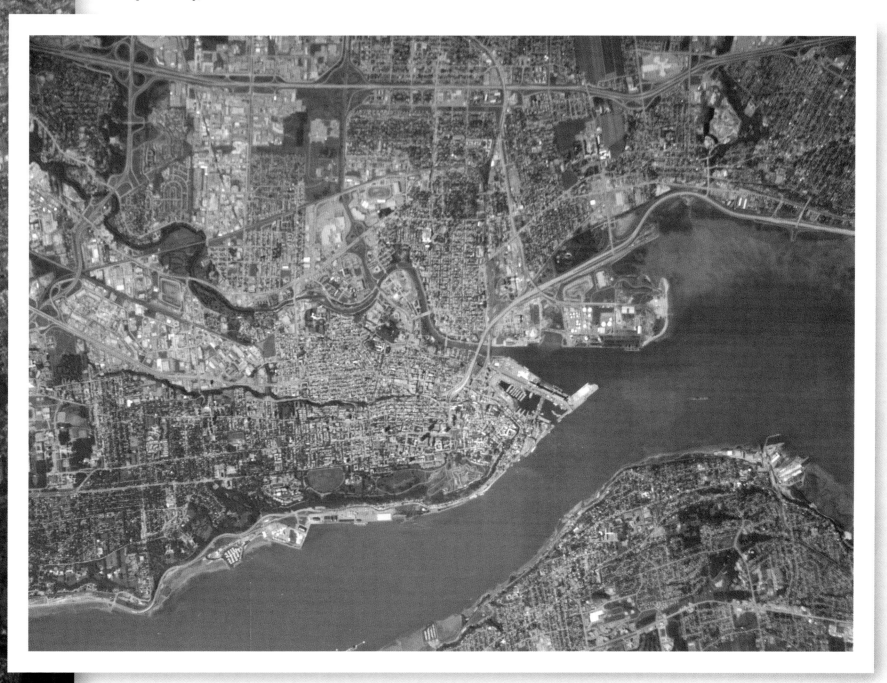

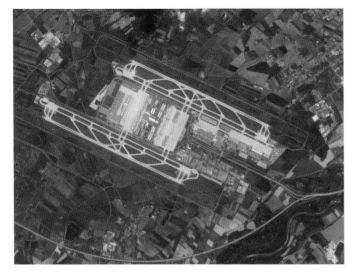

Clockwise from upper left:

Munich Airport in Germany.

Dallas/Fort Worth International Airport in Texas.

Baghdad International Airport, Iraq.

A high concentration of contrails over western Europe are common and reveal the intensive pace of commerce in the region.

Holloman Air Force Base, New Mexico.

This airplane—likely a commercial flight from Asia to the U.S.—can be seen in front of its contrail, flying southeast of Adak Island in Alaska's Aleutian chain.

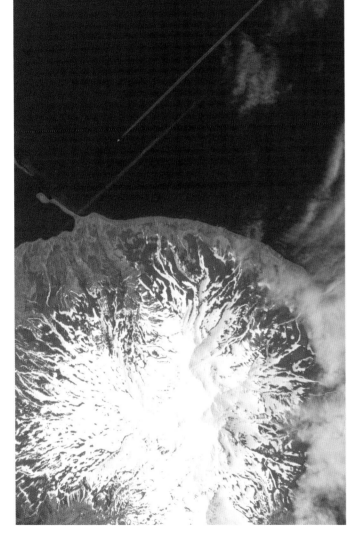

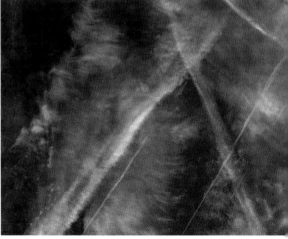

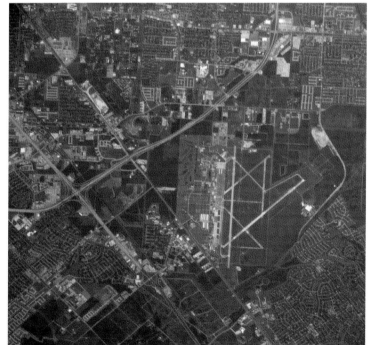

Above: Minneapolis-St. Paul International Airport in Minnesota.

Upper right corner: Edwards Air Force Base, California.

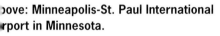

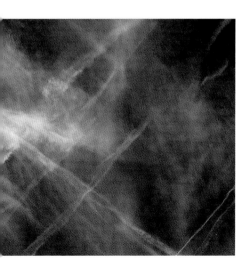

Above: Ellington Field, our home field at Johnson Space Center, in Houston, Texas.

Left: El Paso Airport and the adjacent Biggs Army Airfield in Texas, our base for space shuttle approach training.

109

Left: Port of Baltimore, Maryland.

Confederation Bridge, below, connects Prince Edward Island with the mainland of New Brunswick, Canada. The sixty-two piers supporting the nearly 8-mile bridge produce a unique pattern downstream in the tidal currents easily seen in the sun glint.

Top right: Suez Canal, Egypt.

Bottom right: Long Beach, California, among the busiest ports in the United States.

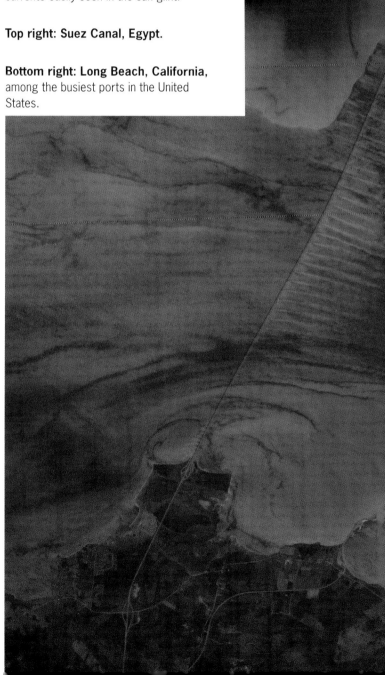

Above: The Ural River Delta and ship channel in eastern Kazakhstan on the Caspian Sea.

Top right: The Brownsville Ship Channel is cut from the Gulf of Mexico about seventeen miles inland to the port of Brownsville, Texas.

Middle: Venice, Italy.

Far right: The Twin Ports of Duluth, Minnesota, and Superior, Wisconsin, are common destinations for the Great Lakes shipping industry.

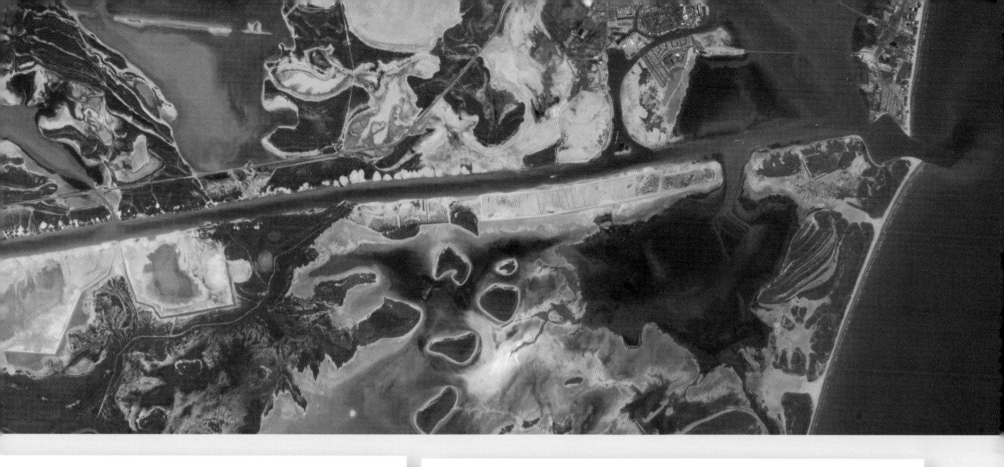

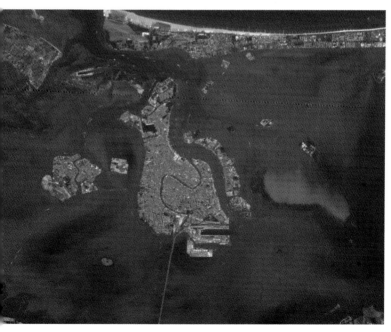

Above: **Milwaukee, Wisconsin.**

Right: Ship channel in the Volga River Delta, Russia, on the Caspian Sea.

Opposite page: Seattle, Washington.

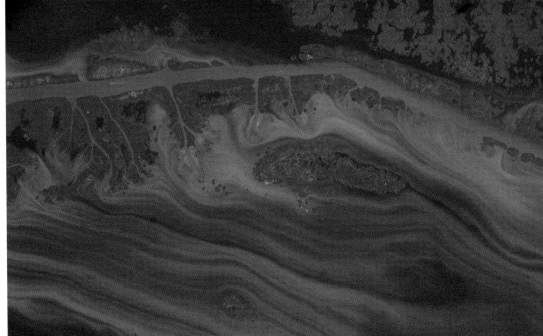

Above: The Nile Delta in Egypt.

Middle: The Egyptian pyramids at Giza—
one of the seven wonders of the ancient world—
are easily viewed with the help of a zoom lens.

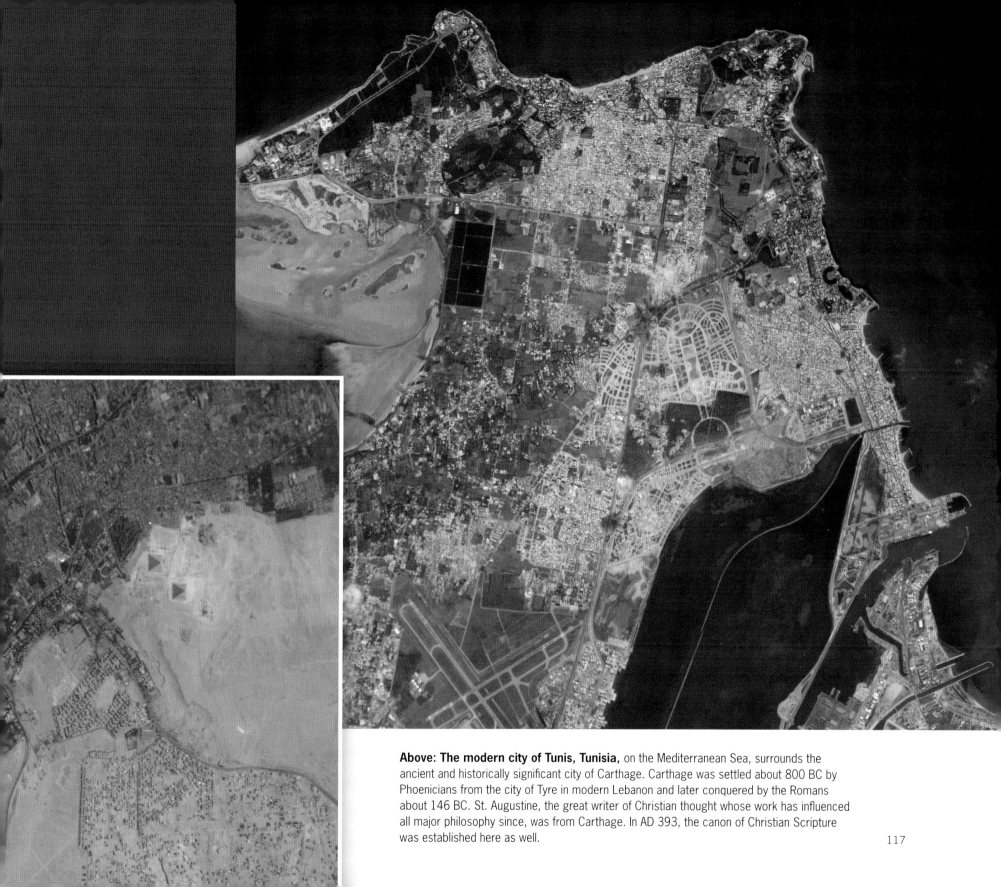

Above: The modern city of Tunis, Tunisia, on the Mediterranean Sea, surrounds the ancient and historically significant city of Carthage. Carthage was settled about 800 BC by Phoenicians from the city of Tyre in modern Lebanon and later conquered by the Romans about 146 BC. St. Augustine, the great writer of Christian thought whose work has influenced all major philosophy since, was from Carthage. In AD 393, the canon of Christian Scripture was established here as well.

117

Above: The Johnston Atoll—located in the South Pacific about 750 nautical miles west of Hawaii—is uninhabited. It was a U.S. Navy Air Station shelled by the Japanese in World War II and later a nuclear weapons test site.

Left: Guantanamo Bay, Cuba.

Above: Pearl Harbor, Hawaii.

9

U.S.-Style Spacewalking

August 1—All continues to go well on board as we approach EVA day. The dry run on Friday went well from a crew perspective and for the ground team. We are making minor adjustments to the procedures and tools, and I feel very comfortable in the preparations.

This space walk will be on more familiar "terrain" than the one Pavel and I conducted on June 1, but there will still be plenty of things new. The more familiar include the U.S. suits (instead of Russian Orlan suits) and working exclusively with Houston Mission Control (instead of Moscow) in English (instead of Russian). The new challenges will be the specific tasks on our plate, using the ISS Joint Airlock instead of the shuttle airlock, and venturing to parts of the ISS I haven't been before.

Thomas Reiter and I had trained for the August space walk on only two occasions about eight months earlier. Despite the long wait, the preparations and studying of the plan in the days leading up to the EVA, combined with being well-adjusted to weightlessness and the space environment, gave us a high level of confidence as we prepared to get in the spacesuits and go outside. It was the third career space walk for each of us. The planned work took us from the very starboard end of the Station to the port side, and involved a variety of tasks— including installing a sophisticated sensor for measuring the static charge of the Station, deploying experiments exposing various materials to the extreme environment of space, and replacing several failed system components.

Thomas and I climbed out of and onto the Space Station in darkness somewhere over Southeast Asia and the southern Pacific. We were well into the first task when the sun came up and illuminated a spectacular view of the Cascades and Canadian Rockies followed by the ten-minute flight over the U.S., ending up with us viewing

Immediate left: German astronaut Thomas Reiter is seen here during the August 3 EVA on the big screen in the Houston Mission Control Center as the flight control team monitors the progress.

Opposite page: The author at work.

121

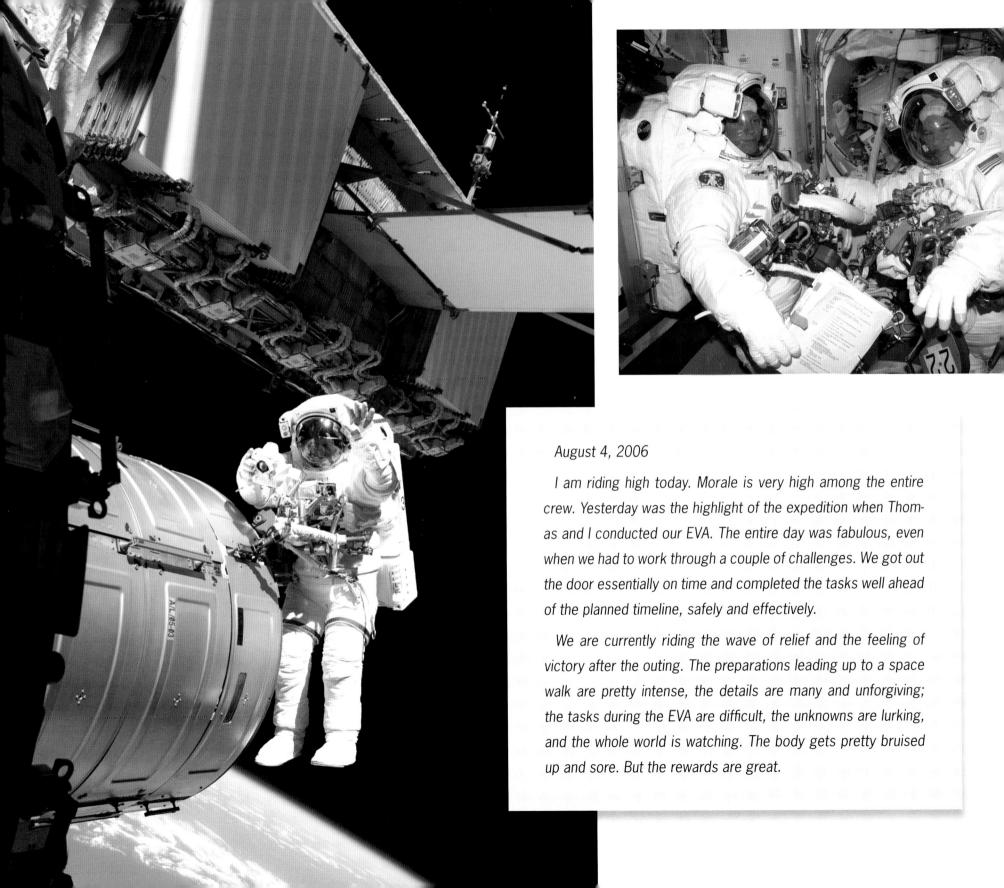

August 4, 2006

I am riding high today. Morale is very high among the entire crew. Yesterday was the highlight of the expedition when Thomas and I conducted our EVA. The entire day was fabulous, even when we had to work through a couple of challenges. We got out the door essentially on time and completed the tasks well ahead of the planned timeline, safely and effectively.

We are currently riding the wave of relief and the feeling of victory after the outing. The preparations leading up to a space walk are pretty intense, the details are many and unforgiving; the tasks during the EVA are difficult, the unknowns are lurking, and the whole world is watching. The body gets pretty bruised up and sore. But the rewards are great.

Florida, where the shuttle *Atlantis* had just arrived at its launch pad the day prior. Later during the space walk, we had two more great passes over the U.S., the first taking us over the Houston area and the next just off the coast of California. After that, our day passes were primarily over the Pacific Ocean with some viewing of South America. The sights were amazing and varied—from the sunrises and sunsets, to lightning and city lights, mesmerizing moon phases, and fabulous cloud formations. At one point while still outside, Pavel called our attention to another spectacular view of noctilucent clouds over Antarctica—those rarely seen and mysterious high clouds I wrote about previously.

Job says God "hangs the earth on nothing" (26:7). Seeing the entire planet from outside punctuated Job's witness with indescribable significance. Job's conclusion that all of creation is but "outskirts of His ways" (26:14) was especially humbling and only increased my wonder and awe of the Creator.

10

The Provision of Earth

From space, it is obvious that Earth was made to sustain life—human life—and that mankind has been an industrious tenant. The scope, cycles, patterns, and colors of agriculture disclose a wide array of information even to a distant observer. Hints of climates, seasons, crop types, and irrigation methods are evident. Even cultural, political, and historical dimensions are reflected in the appearance of the agriculture.

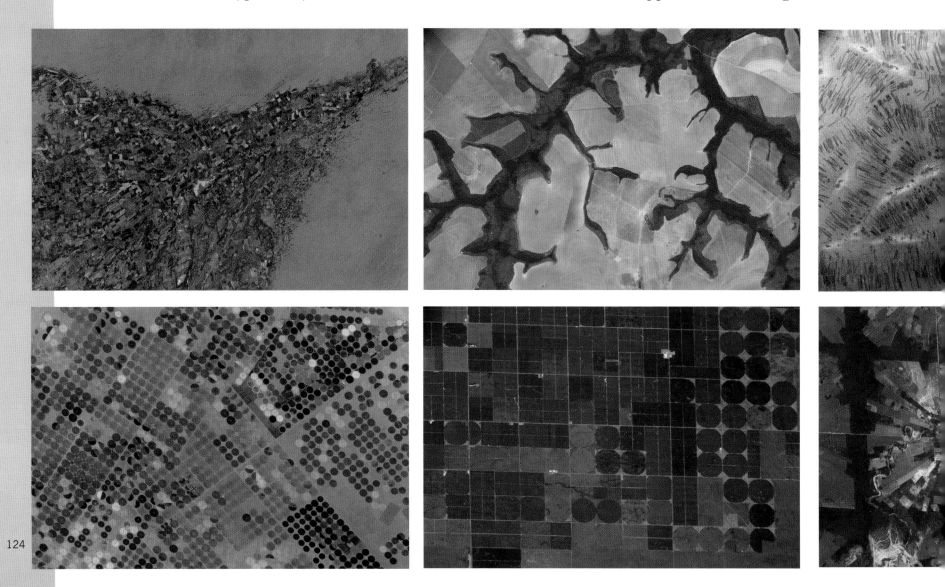

[Lord,] You cause
the grass to grow
for the livestock and
plants for man to cultivate,
that he may bring forth
food from the earth.

Psalm 104:14

Gezira Scheme is a massive irrigation project in Sudan, southeast of the confluence of the Blue and White Nile rivers near Khartoum. Water from the Blue Nile is distributed through a network of canals with a total length of 2,700 miles. Cotton is the primary crop in this region.

While acknowledging the reality of problems with food shortages and crises throughout history, the provision that comes from the natural components and conditions of the earth—soil, water, seed, climate, and seasons—is amazing. Even more amazing are the God-given abilities of mankind to extract from the earth crops for food and other uses.

That provision and those abilities give testimony to the wisdom and graciousness of God as the Sustainer of His creation. It has been said that God *hides* Himself in creation. He hides Himself behind the giving, sustaining, and providential care, as well as the abilities of mankind, and they give testimony to Him.

The many evidences of the history, the continuous activities of different cultures, and the obvious signs of utilization in that provision from the earth are reminders of the stamp of the Creator on mankind while

Pictures on p. 124, top row, left to right:
Unique agricultural patterns located in Turkmenistan along the Murghab River and surrounded by the Karakum Desert. One of several reservoirs reflects sunlight in the center of the photograph.

Along the darker river beds, contours are easily seen in the distinctive patterns and colors characteristic of Brazilian agriculture.

Linear agriculture patterns in Ethiopia.

Pictures on p. 124, bottom row, left to right:
Center-pivot irrigation supports agriculture and covers vast areas of desert in Saudi Arabia. The development of such techniques was accelerated in the 1970s and 1980s. Water for irrigation primarily comes from deep wells.

The midwest and western plains display an agricultural pattern of one-square-mile parcels (known as sections), revealing a piece of history in the settling of the United States. The Homestead Act of 1862 provided for a transfer of 160 acres or one quarter

also giving us a glimpse of what it means to bear the image of God. Human creativity is evident in the discovery, development, and utilization of natural resources, raw materials, and energy sources found in, on, from, and around Earth. That creativity is a direct extension of God's original creative work recorded in the Book of Genesis. Creative activity found in humankind, God's creatures, not only gives evidence of His wisdom and the image we bear, but that creativity directly glorifies the God of creation. When we look at the creative accomplishments—past and ongoing—across the spectrum of human activity, we see God at work through us and in us. In that way, He is reflected in us. Those accomplishments stretch from the most basic activities of agriculture for sustenance to the on-orbit assembly of the International Space Station, and everything in between.

of a section to a homesteader for $1.25 per acre. Multiple sections defined townships, the boundaries for school systems and the jurisdiction of local government. In this photo, sections (or one square mile) are evident in the square pattern of roads marking out the section boundaries. Smaller divisions down to forty acre plots are visible in the irrigation and agricultural contrasts.

Forestry activity in the Tierras Bajas Project in eastern Bolivia. Agricultural pinwheel patterns radiate out from small communities, spaced at 5 kilometer intervals.

Pictures on pp. 126–27, left to right: **French agriculture; Irrigation** in the midwestern United States. The variety of colors indicates different crops, harvested areas, or, perhaps, quarter sections lying fallow; **Rich agricultural region** of eastern Ukraine; **Neglected or abandoned fields** in southern Iraq; **The patterns and colors** of this agricultural region are unique to northern France, a region rich in the production of cereal grains; and **Brazilian agriculture.**

Northern France The Somme River flows out over a broad estuary into the English Channel. Surrounded by a patchwork of agriculture, the area in view was the site of one of the largest battles of World War I.

Below: Cerignola, Italy This old Italian city was originally a stop on an ancient Roman road. Notice the radial roads and surrounding agriculture.

Right: Modena, Italy The dense center of the ancient Roman city is surrounded by the agriculture of north central Italy.

Above: A river meanders in northern Louisiana.

Top left: Nile River Delta in Egypt Highlighted by sur
the intricate structures along the coast are fisheries. Kr
aquiculture, this industry was made possible by the Asw
Dam. Before the building of the Aswan High Dam in the
seasonal floods made such commercial ventures impos

Top right: Western Qinghai province of China The
is centered at 36.9 N, 95.3 E in the Qarhan salt flats. T
structures appear to be sediment ponds, perhaps for th
production of potash.

Left: More salt sediment ponds in China.

Opposite page: The Axios River Delta near Thessal
Greece.

131

The provision of Earth goes well beyond agriculture. History and even the names of historical periods testify to the richness of the planet's resources and mankind's search for, development, and use of those resources. History labels periods by such names as the Bronze Age, the Iron Age, and the Industrial Age. Economics and commerce in history have been largely driven by what the earth provides. In history, exploration has been motivated by such things as spices, silk, and gold. Viewing Earth from space reflects that history.

I came to appreciate the richness of the earth and being a steward of those riches as a young boy. Growing up on a dairy farm, I saw firsthand what the land provided, the cycles of life and seasons, and the disciplined labor required to extract the land's benefits. Later, as a teenager working as a carpenter, I grew in appreciation for the resources enabling so much around us and which we take for granted: trees for the wide array of lumber products; the raw materials for concrete, steel, aluminum, copper, and other metals; water; electricity; and much more. That experience became a backdrop as I searched for examples of mining the earth.

This page, top: The checkerboard pattern in parts of Washington state reveals the method of harvesting lumber, apparently by section. Directly below, we see **the same checkerboard pattern** in parts of Washington state before the spring snow melt.

Facing page, clockwise from top left: Boron mine north of Edwards Air Force Base in the Mojave Desert.

An open-pit copper mine in northern Mexico adjacent to the city of Cananea.

The Argyle diamond mine located in northwestern Australia.

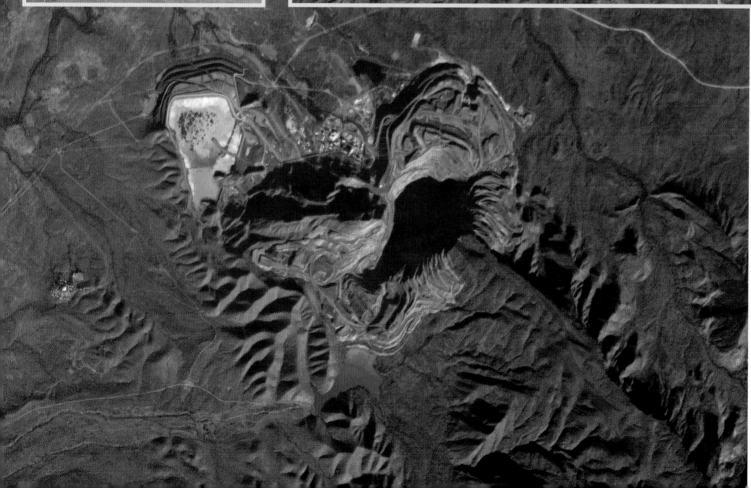

A calcite quarry in the Upper Peninsula of Michigan.

Surely there is a mine for silver,
and a place for gold that they refine.
Iron is taken out of the earth,
and copper is smelted from the ore.

Job 28:1–2

Right: Once an underground mine, the Berkeley Pit, adjacent to Butte, MT, was nicknamed "The Richest Hill on Earth" in the late 1800s. Although some silver and gold were mined, copper was the prominent ore produced after 1955 when the pit was opened. Visible are the terraced sides of the pit, the adjacent tailings pond (left), and the pit itself (dark area). Although the mine appears active here, it was closed in 1982. Since then, underground aquifers have filled the pit. The water in the pit is more than 900 feet deep. The water is also toxic from heavy metals and other contaminants.

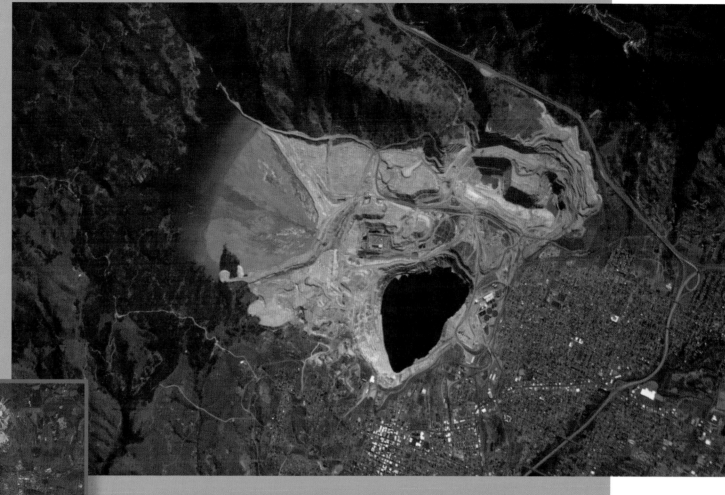

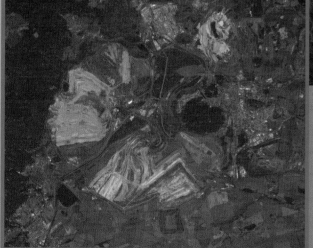

Above: Large, open-pit lignite (brown coal) mining near Most, Czech Republic, can be seen here adjacent to agricultural and wooded areas.

Right: The Rosebud coal mine near Colstrip, MT.

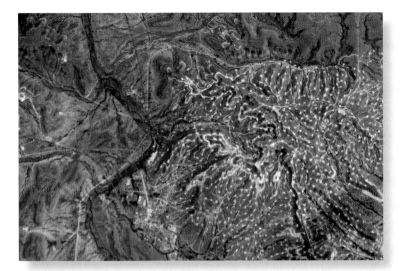

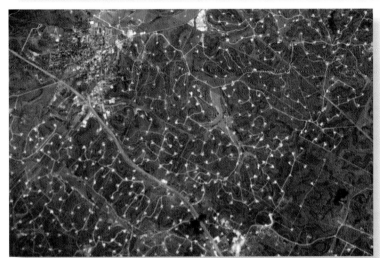

Left column: Yates Oilfield, located in West Texas, with Pecos River bed in view.

A West Texas oil field.

Solar arrays in Southern California.

Above: Oil wells in the midst of irrigation circles in eastern New Mexico.

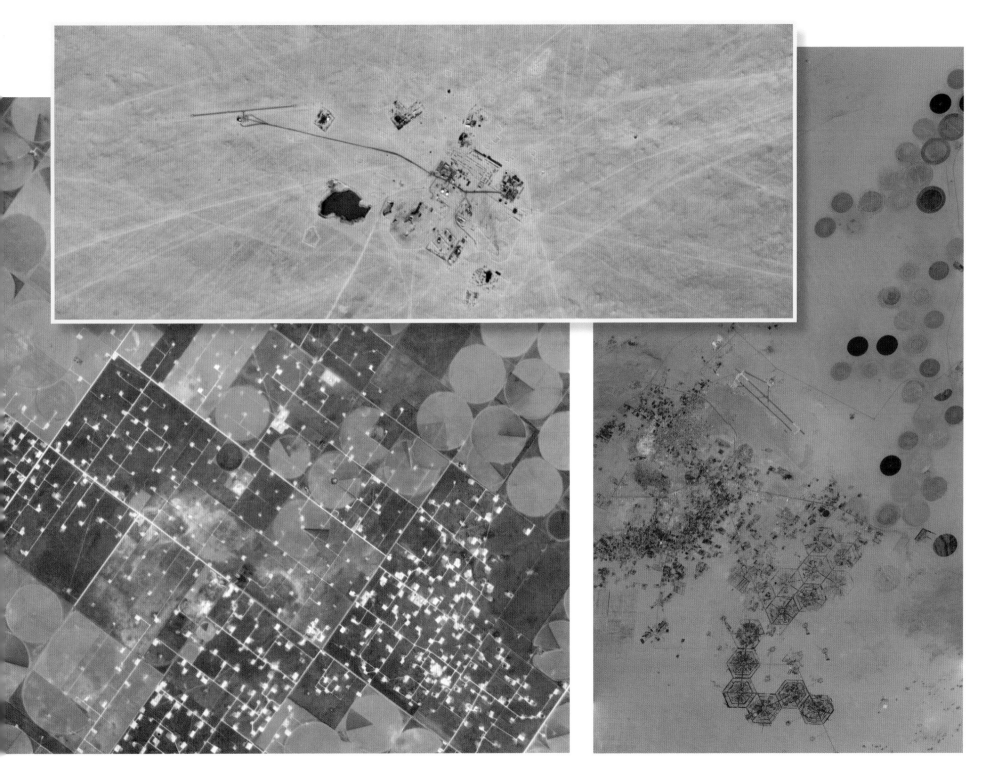

Top: A remote base—perhaps an oil field—located in northeastern Libya at 29 N, 20.7 E. Note the desert roads radiating in all directions.

Far right: Kufra is an isolated oasis located in the middle of the Sahara desert in eastern Libya.

11

Dynamic Events

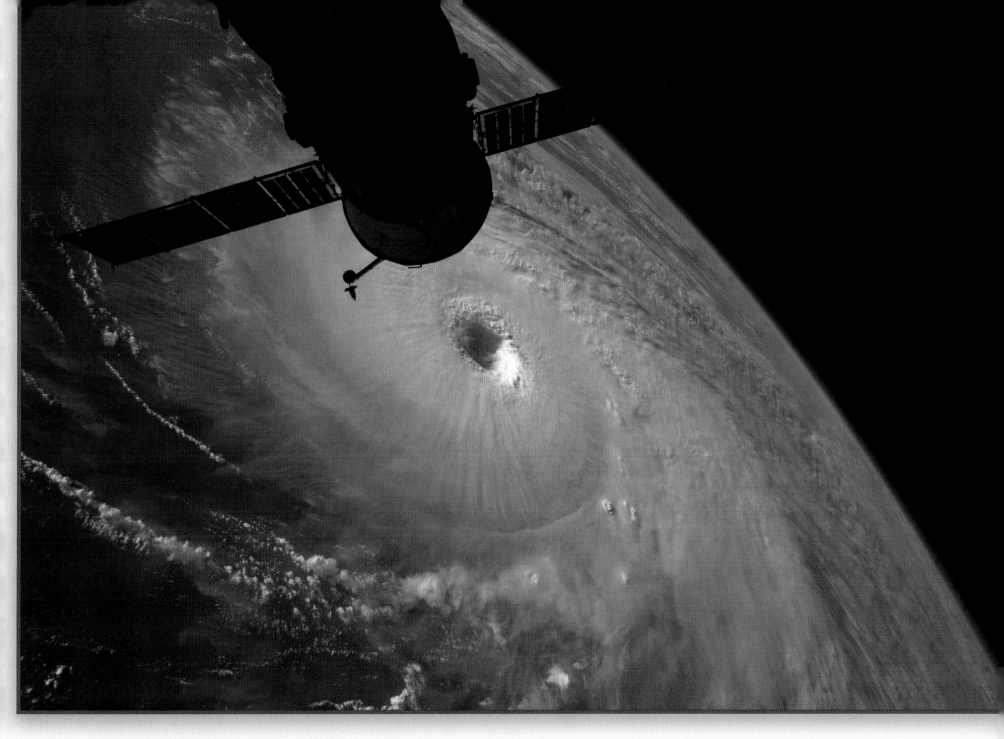

Left page: Photographed on August 14, 2006, a huge plume of volcanic ash and smoke is visible in this oblique view of the Ubinas Volcano, one of the most active volcanoes in Peru.

Above: Category 3 Hurricane Gordon over the Atlantic Ocean, September 14, 2006.

Although life on Earth can appear static as the International Space Station passes over a portion of the Earth's surface, some sightings are obviously anything but, and I have collected a few examples in this section. They include photography of dynamic occurrences such as fires, volcanic activity, sandstorms, and weather systems. Some events were of relatively short duration, others lasted for days or weeks; some had relatively local impact, others appeared to be widespread. The observed events, even from such a distance, were spectacular and, in their own right, beautiful. Had we not been receiving news reports from the planet—reports of the destruction, terror, injury, or death associated with what we were viewing—we might have continued to admire the strange beauty on display in these events.

Beginning at the top left photo, this enormous panoramic photo follows the Missouri River as smoke plumes from forest fires collected to form a haze over the entire western half of North America late in the summer of 2006. Here, multiple forest fires—likely started by lightning storms—burn on the south shore of the Missouri River and Fort Peck Lake in eastern Montana on July 16, 2006. These photos were taken looking south while the ISS flew over Alberta, Canada, to the northwest.

War in Lebanon: We received periodic news updates on board the ISS, and I would attempt to capture observations of current events. Knowing a war was raging between Israel and Hezbollah, I shot a series of photographs on August 1, 2006, while passing over southern Lebanon. Here, a plume of smoke rises from the Jiyyeh power plant located between Beirut and Saida after the latest in a series of bombings.

Opposite page, clockwise from top left: Sandstorms in eastern Kazakhstan.

The huge plume from the Day Fire burning in southern California rises over the Los Padres National Forest on September 4, 2006. The fire started on Labor Day and was not contained for well over a month.

A sandstorm in northern Kazakhstan.

This huge fire in southern Ontario, on July 1, 2006, sent smoke high into the atmosphere.

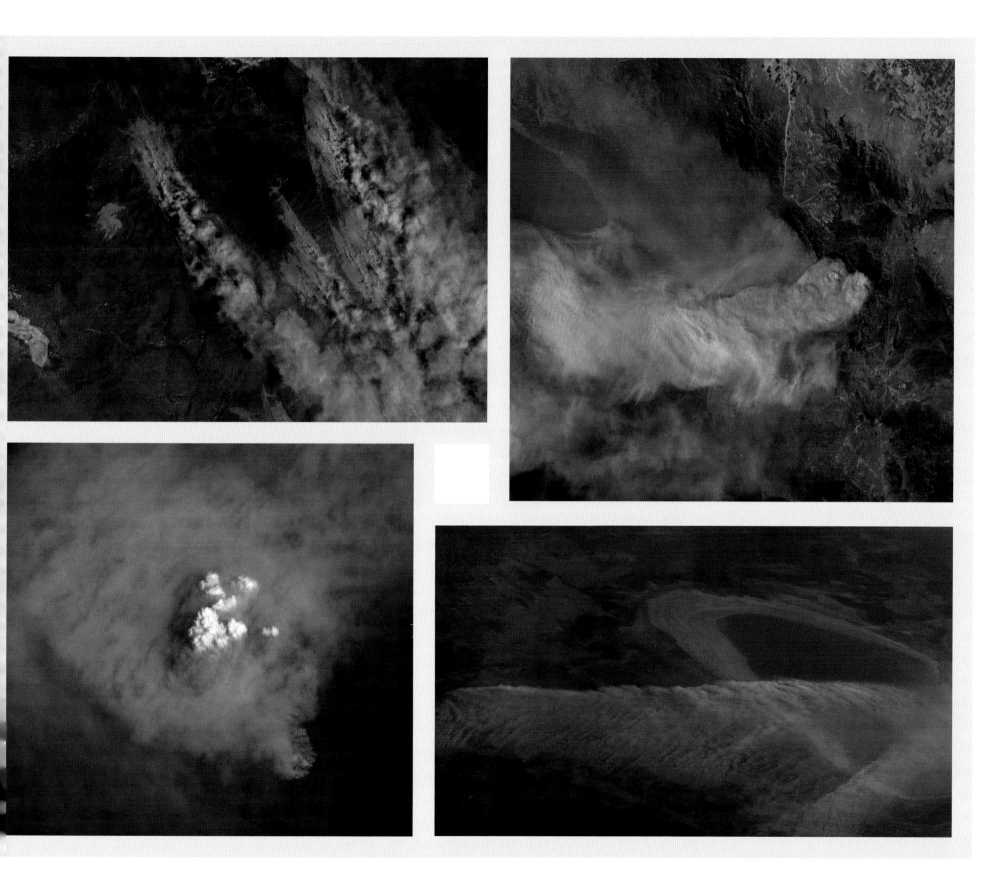

Continuing the Assembly—High-Rise Construction

After several weather delays, STS-115 and the crew of *Atlantis* launched from Kennedy Space Center on September 9 and docked two days later. Upon getting the hatches open, we welcomed veteran astronauts Brent Jett, Joe Tanner, Dan Burbank, and Steve MacLean, and first-time flyers Chris Ferguson and Heidi Stefanyshyn-Piper. Once again, it was great to see friends from the planet below.

The mission was another significant milestone in resuming the major assembly of the ISS after the *Columbia* tragedy and return to flight of the space shuttle program. The *Atlantis* crew's primary task was to deliver, install, and activate a major truss element of the external ISS systems. The element, referred to as the P3 and P4 truss segments, featured large solar arrays, batteries, and other associated equipment integrated into it. Those components are used to produce electrical power to run the Station. The new segments would provide power for the international laboratory modules to be added later. The segments added about 45 feet to the structural truss across the back of the Station, bringing the span to about 240 feet.

The primary activities performed during STS-115 included complicated robotic operations to install the P3/P4 truss elements and three space walks—two by Tanner and Piper and one by Burbank and MacLean—to complete the power system activation. All operations were successful. With the completion of the *Atlantis* mission and their undocking on September 17, the ISS looked markedly different with the new components in place. The way was cleared for the arrival of our relief.

September 12

We are almost through our first full day with Atlantis docked. So far the mission is going like clockwork. Docking day went as expected, and we got off to a great start yesterday. Steve and I got the P3/P4 truss elements installed this morning, and Joe and Heidi are nearing the completion of EVA 1. There is a flurry of activity going on and everybody is doing very well. It's great to have them on board and a great way to finish out Expedition 13.

Candid shot of several crew members in the *Unity* module during STS-115.

Atlantis departs from the ISS with an empty payload bay.

12

The Work of His Hands

When I look at Your heavens, the work of Your fingers,
the moon and the stars, which You have set in place,
what is man that You are mindful of him? Psalm 8:3–4

The whole of creation is manifest with beauty and wonder, and with evidence of the Creator. But the creation provides but a glimpse—that "small whisper" described in Job 26—of God, who is the Creator. When people see Earth from the perspective of orbit, whether firsthand or through the descriptions of those who have been there, their thoughts often turn to God, or at least the question of God.

I often get asked questions such as: "Do you feel closer to God up there?" or "Has the experience changed your faith or belief in God?" It may come as a surprise that I answer the questions no—with a caveat.

Anna-Marie and I have a strong Christian faith that had its beginning in the late 1980s, and we labor to live accordingly. Over the years of studying the Bible, I have grown both in awe of it and in complete trust in it as the source of the truth of reality, wisdom, and all things necessary for life. I have also come to realize we can only know *about* God by viewing creation, irrespective of our vantage point. It is only through the revelation of God in the Scriptures that we can actually become close to Him in relationship and actually *know* Him. This is God's most profound gracious provision to us.

No, my experiences as an astronaut did not bring me closer to God or change my beliefs about His existence. My relationship with God does not hinge on my looking at Earth from orbit and experiencing that "small whisper" that is so evident in creation. True, life-transforming faith in God and relationship with Him is based not on a *whisper*, but a *shout*—the shout of God's Son, the Lord Jesus Christ, in His work on the cross as revealed in the supernatural revelation of the Bible. So my closeness to God in relationship with Him is through faith in the person and work of Christ.

With that said, the experience did have an impact. My faith was already established through the objective means of His written Word and its Gospel message. The experience of being on the Space Station only intensified the content of the Word and my response to it as I viewed the work of His fingers (Psalm 8) through the lens of the Bible in a special way. That response occurred in ways I will attempt to explain.

I was able to reflect on God as *Creator* in a fresh way. The wonder and awe of viewing all of the elements of Earth from orbit was overpowering. Some have heard me speak of the beauty of the blue planet, of the vastness of the oceans and varied landforms, the magnificent cloud formations and water currents, the wonder of lightning storms stretching over a thousand miles, and the dazzling light display of the aurora over the poles. The relative thinness of the atmosphere that provides for life, the day-night cycles, and the beauty of the atmosphere during sunrises or sunsets are also vivid memories. Viewing all of those things intensified for me the meaning of passages such as Job 26:7, 10: "He stretches out the north over the void and hangs the earth on nothing. . . . He has inscribed a circle on the face of the waters at the boundary between light and darkness." Psalm 8:3–4 speaks of the humility that comes when one considers creation: "When I look at Your heavens, the work of Your fingers . . . ." The view from orbit was humbling in ways well beyond previous experience. And Psalm 19 is among my favorites because it speaks of how creation reveals God's existence but how He is only fully revealed in His Word.

The experience on the Space Station also intensified my faith by helping me consider God's providence and governing of His creation—that is, God as the *Sustainer* and *Provider*. *Providence* is a term not used much in modern times, but I love the richness of it. The reality of God's providence transcended the entire experience of Expedition 13. Psalm 139 speaks to providence and the manifestation of God's ever-present care, and verses 9–10 took on special meaning: "If I take the wings of the morning and dwell in the uttermost parts of the sea, even there Your hand shall lead me, and Your right hand shall hold me." In Colossians 1:16–17, Christ is acknowledged as the Creator and also the one who sustains—that is upholds and governs—His creation. While in orbit for six months, I grew in appreciation of being sustained and upheld day by day.

Of course, the special revelation found in the Scriptures climaxes in the redemption of sinners—that is, God as *Redeemer*. And that redeeming work is found in the person and work of Jesus Christ—the good news of the Gospel. That reality of God as *Redeemer* also became more vivid from the spaceflight experience as a direct result of the deepened perspectives of God as *Creator, Sustainer, and Provider*.

Far right top: The region of the seven churches of Asia Minor addressed by John in Revelation 2–3 are seen here in what today is the western portion of Turkey.

Far right bottom: The Aegean Sea with Greece on the left and top, and eastern Turkey on the right. Many of the apostle Paul's stops on his second and third journeys, recorded in Acts 16–20, are in view.

152

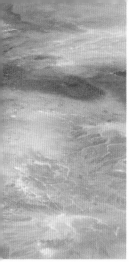

Long ago, at many times and in many ways,
God spoke to our fathers by the prophets, but
in these last days He has spoken to us by His Son,
whom He appointed the heir of all things, through
whom also He created the world. He is the
radiance of the glory of God and the exact
imprint of His nature, and He upholds the universe
by the word of His power. *Hebrews 1:1–3a*

In hindsight, I have come to realize anew that viewing and living out life through that lens intensifies the trust, confidence, and sense of contentment that come in living out our faith in even the most challenging times. That perspective also invokes an intense humility and grows gratitude. It causes one to slow a bit and contemplate life issues in a new way. Additionally, it magnifies the sense of responsibility and stewardship that comes with getting such an experience. I have an obligation to share the experience and bring it back to those on Earth.

With all of that in mind, among my favorite portions of the Earth to observe was the Middle East. The significance of redemptive history recorded in the Bible was brought to mind when I could see, in a single panorama, the entire area in which it took place. All of that history—from Abraham to Moses to David, the birth, life, death, and resurrection of Jesus Christ, and the subsequent journeys and work of the apostles in the spreading of the Gospel—was, in a sense, made visible in a fresh, tangible way when the biblical lands were in view out the window. I know I will never look at the maps in the back of my Bible the same way.

Clockwise from top left: Damascus, Syria; the Jordan Valley; the Sinai Peninsula; oblique view of Middle East This view captures the area where much of biblical history occurred, including the life of Abraham, the exodus of the Israelites and their entrance into the Promised Land, the United—and later Divided—Kingdom of Israel, as well as the life of Jesus.

Homeward Bound

13

By mid-September, Expedition 13 was coming to a close. Most mission objectives were behind us, safely accomplished by the team. The team, including the flight and ground crew, had grown to be a family with a high level of trust, loyalty, and dedication to one another. We commemorated that relationship one day by posing with those on our ground team on the big screen in the Mission Control Center. Ultimately, the people made the experience for me and it was an honor to be part of such a group.

The final phase of the mission came with the arrival of the relief crew for Pavel and me: U.S. astronaut Michael Lopez-Alegria and Russian cosmonaut Mikhail Tyurin. They came to join Thomas Reiter and begin Expedition 14. Launching just a few hours after STS-115 had undocked and departed, Lopez-Alegria and Tyurin, along with spaceflight participant Anousheh Ansari, spent the better part of two days confined inside the tiny Soyuz spacecraft catching up to the ISS. Our anticipation of their arrival brought forth the same high-spirited and joyful response in us that we had seen six months earlier in the crew we relieved. It was a bittersweet time, knowing we would soon be reunited with our families, while, at the same time, leaving behind our crewmate Thomas Reiter, our temporary home, and the unique environment of space.

September 28 – I depart the Station with full satisfaction with what we accomplished and how we accomplished it. It has been a reward of complete fulfillment both professionally and personally. No major issues were encountered. In fact, no minor issues were encountered. The crew interaction on board was near perfect, as was the interaction among the on-board crew and the ground teams. As in all aspects of this experience, I count it first and foremost a manifestation of God's grace to us. His faithful provision to endure came day by day, and day by day I faced the challenge. That provision came, in part, through the means of many faithful friends and family. His providence continues to amaze me. Gratitude overwhelms me. I am content and at peace. In His service and for His glory, Jeff

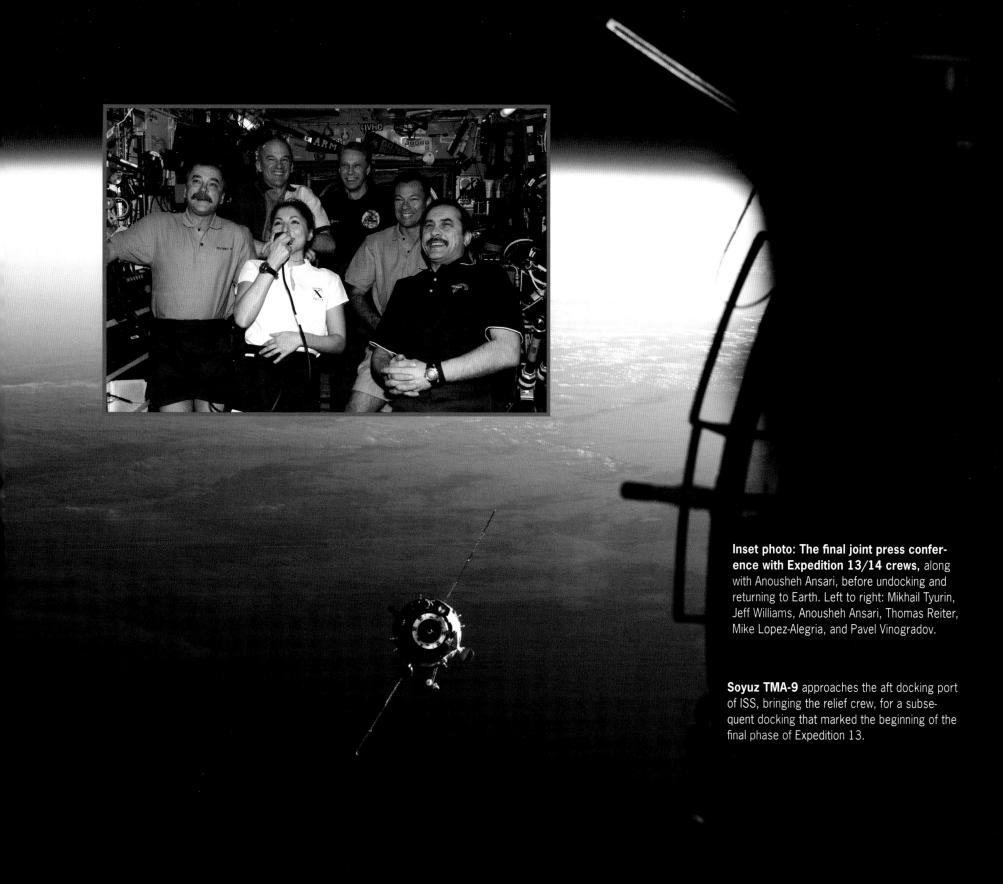

Inset photo: The final joint press conference with Expedition 13/14 crews, along with Anousheh Ansari, before undocking and returning to Earth. Left to right: Mikhail Tyurin, Jeff Williams, Anousheh Ansari, Thomas Reiter, Mike Lopez-Alegria, and Pavel Vinogradov.

Soyuz TMA-9 approaches the aft docking port of ISS, bringing the relief crew, for a subsequent docking that marked the beginning of the final phase of Expedition 13.

The Houston Mission Control Center team poses for a group photo with the ISS Expedition 13 crew on the screen in the background via live video downlink.

With the successful docking and ingress of the Expedition 14 crew, we began the eight-day handover, reviewing the Station's systems and on-going operations. The handover culminated in the traditional change of command ceremony the day prior to undocking. Then, our efforts shifted toward preparing our Soyuz spacecraft and ourselves for the return to the planet below.

The success of Expedition 13 was due, in large part, to the dedicated and extremely talented crew on

Williams and Lopez-Alegria conducting robotic operations during the handover period.

the ground: the Mission Control Teams in Houston, Huntsville, Munich, and Moscow; and the much larger teams composed of technicians, engineers, managers, medical staff, administrative staff, and others spread across the entire international partnership of governments and contractors. Thousands of people dedicated to the mission—safe and effective space exploration—are responsible for the success of the human endeavor we call the International Space Station.

Undocking

The time from undocking the Soyuz TMA-8 spacecraft from the ISS until touchdown on Earth was only about four and a half hours. During the day of our departure, there was an intense feeling of time compression on the Station. While the previous months seemed to crawl by day to day, now the minutes raced by as we completed the final stowage of last-minute payloads, said our farewells, floated into the Soyuz, closed the hatch, and prepared for undocking.

For entry—like ascent and docking—the Soyuz crew wears pressure suits in case a capsule leak were to occur during the dynamic phases of deorbit and entry. After donning the suits, we floated into our seats and closed the hatch between the descent module—where we would remain protected by the heat shield during entry—and the habitation module, which would later burn up in the atmosphere. To prepare for undocking, we worked exclusively with Moscow Mission Control, just as we did with the launch, ascent, rendezvous, and docking. All communications were solely in Russian.

After pressure-integrity checks and readying the Soyuz systems, undocking occurred with a slight bump, followed by our spacecraft slowly drifting away from the Space Station. The next three and a half hours were relatively quiet as we prepared for the precise moment for the deorbit firing of the main engine that would bring us to the targeted and predictable landing site. The search-and-rescue forces—equipped with airplanes, helicopters, and all-terrain vehicles—were already staged in the areas of both the prime and contingency landing sites.

Deorbit burn

Landing in the right place on the planet requires firing the main engine (deorbit burn) at precisely the right point in precisely the right spacecraft orientation for precisely the right amount of time. Many critical steps are required of the crew to prepare and execute this maneuver. For many maneuvers, telemetry to Mission Control through ground communication sites allows the ground team to assist and "look over the shoulder" of the flight crew. The flight crew is on its own for deorbit because there is no communication with the ground during that phase.

Wearing the Sokol pressure suit, Williams gets situated in the left seat of the descent module in preparation for undocking and returning to earth. Note the porthole window to his left, through which he later watched the fireball of entry and eventually saw soil and grass a few inches outside the window. The cloth-covered bundles to the left contain survival equipment for use if entry resulted in landing off-target.

Soyuz TMA-8 drifting away from the ISS after undocking.

In the minutes leading up to the burn, time sped up again. We activated and readied the systems and maneuvered the spacecraft to the proper orientation. The engine ignited at precisely the correct time as we flew over the South Pacific, settling us into our seats under the acceleration of less than half the force of gravity, and burned for exactly 4 minutes and 20 seconds without any issues.

About 20 minutes after the deorbit burn, pyrotechnic bolts connecting the descent module to the habitation module and engine compartment fired with an explosive bang. Our descent module was separated from the habitation module and the engine compartment, leaving the three components flying in formation on a trajectory toward an entry into the atmosphere.

Entry and Touchdown

A few minutes after the separation of the modules, the force of acceleration (or g-load) began to build. We were still on the night side of the earth when a faint orange glow appeared around us, visible in the windows. The glow—not from the sun—became brighter and brighter, and it was apparent that we were in a fireball of intense heat caused by the friction as we entered the upper atmosphere at such a high velocity. The g-loading also

Because we landed just at sunrise, there are no pictures of Soyuz TMA-8 landing. But here you can see the Soyuz TMA-9 spacecraft floating to a landing southwest of Karaganda, Kazakhstan, on April 21, 2007.

continued to increase and peaked at about 4 times the force of gravity (feeling 4 times our body weight while lying on our backs), after which it rapidly decreased. The seat design conformed to our backs, and since we were descending back first, the high loads were very tolerable.

After a few minutes of intense heating outside and the high loads of acceleration, the next phase was initiated automatically. With a loud explosion, the drogue parachute deployed, causing another period of high loading with moderate shaking and oscillation. The main parachute deployed seconds later and, after the opening shock and the explosive jettisoning of the thermal shield seconds later, the sense of motions settled down until we were hanging quietly under the fully deployed parachute. A few minutes after that, our seats automatically stroked up a few inches, extending a shock absorber designed to protect us from the impact on the ground to come.

Hanging safely under the deployed parachute, all we could do was float down and wait for the impact. We knew we were on target for the landing site when a radio call came to us from the search-and-rescue airplane. That call came immediately after the parachute deployed. They had us in sight and began calling our altitudes so we could anticipate impact. They also directed the helicopters to our point of touchdown.

Touchdown was just like the description of previous crews. The soft-landing thrusters ("soft" is a misnomer) under the capsule fired automatically just prior to impact about 4 feet off the ground. Inside the capsule, it sounded like a very large explosion. The impulse of the thrusters and the impact with the ground was a single jolt. Imagine a car wreck, and that's what the landing felt like. But the seats and custom seat liners did their job perfectly and we came to rest, unscathed.

We landed at 13:13 UTC a little more than fifty miles north of Arkalyk, Kazakhstan, marking the end of a flight lasting 182 days, 23 hours, and 44 minutes. It was at sunrise and the outside temperature was just above freezing.

14

Back Home on Earth—
Mission Complete

Lord, You have been faithful and brought us through a most remarkable experience and to a safe reunion with our families. Your daily provision and providential care was abundant and amazing and gave testimony to your grace. For that, we are grateful. Amen.

Above: Search-and-rescue forces surround the descent module shortly after landing.

Left: Anousheh Ansari, Pavel Vinogradov, and Jeff Williams.

Within seconds of the impact on the ground and the jettison of the parachute, everything became still. We reported to the search-and-rescue team that we were all fine. The capsule was lying on its side in an orientation that put us on our left side.

Looking out the round window inches from my left shoulder revealed dry grass and dirt just outside, illuminated by the rising sun. Seeing the grass and soil brought an overwhelming feeling of relief and, without saying them aloud, the words came to the forefront of my mind: "We're home!" That feeling came even though we were still halfway around the world in the middle of nowhere. It was similar to the feeling you get when you finally pull into the driveway after a long cross-country trip, only more intense. We were safely back on the planet, "home!"

Within minutes, we could hear a helicopter landing nearby. Then, I could see legs and boots approaching. The boots stopped close to the capsule and a very excited, smiling face and waving hands suddenly appeared in the window; then another and another. Soon, there was a crowd swarming around the still-hot capsule, and we could hear them working on opening the hatch. Finally, when the hatch slowly opened, it was filled with the smiling and familiar face of veteran cosmonaut Sasha Poleshchuk.

The recovery team helped us out one by one from the capsule. Pavel went first, then Anousheh, and finally me. After all that time in weightlessness, gravity had returned to us with a vengeance. They carried us to nearby reclining chairs and wrapped us in fur blankets. The outside temperature was barely

above freezing, but we were still warm inside the suits so the cool air felt good. The breeze blew slightly as the new-day sun shone on the horizon. The air smelled different than inside the spacecraft. In the sterile environment of the Space Station, I had not smelled vegetation and dirt for six months, so it was very noticeable now. The most refreshing sensation was the *quiet*. After six months of being immersed in the continuous drone of fans and pumps, behind the chatter of the recovery team was a refreshing quiet.

Once settled into the chairs, somebody handed me a water bottle and an apple, which I eagerly accepted. The medical team hovered over us, taking blood pressure and measuring our pulse and oxygen levels. We were quizzed on how we were feeling. Though physically exhausted, I have never felt so tranquil. The mission was accomplished, everybody was safe, the years of traveling and months on orbit were complete, and soon my wife, Anna-Marie, and I would be reunited to resume normal life. While we were still sitting in the chairs, somebody offered me a satellite phone. Anna-Marie—relieved and watching from a warm cottage in Star City—was on the other end. It was a very happy conversation.

Shortly thereafter, we were carried to a hastily erected medical tent and were able to get out of our pressure suits and into regular flight suits. It was then that I first stood up under my own power and felt the weight of gravity on my legs and back. Between my lost muscle tone and the yet-confused vestibular system, standing and maintaining balance was a challenge. Aided, we each walked to our own helicopter for an hour flight to a small airport. Local dignitaries and media were waiting there and, following a brief ceremony and press conference, we boarded an airplane for a three and half hour flight back to Star City. Though we had been awake over twenty hours, we spent the time on the airplane relaxing, in conversation with the recovery team and each other about the whole experience. Coming off the airplane, we were finally reunited with our families and greeted by U.S. and Russian government dignitaries. Soon, the entourage was hurried onto a bus and we traveled to the crew quarters to rest. The regimen of physical rehabilitation and debriefings started the next day, and after three weeks, we flew home to Houston for the final stage of homecoming, bringing the thirteenth expedition to the International Space Station to a close.

Williams talking to his wife, Anna-Marie,
via satellite phone shortly after landing.

Postscript

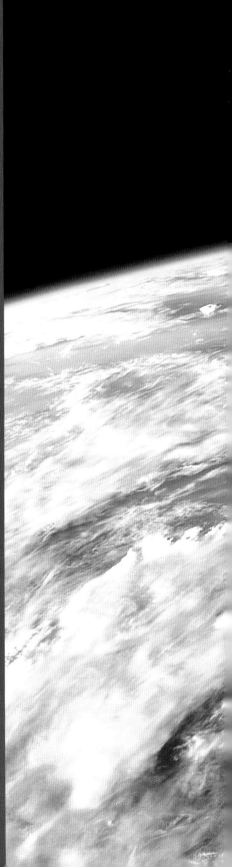

We shall not cease from exploration, and in the end of all our exploring, will be to arrive where we started, and know the place for the first time. —T. S. Elliot, Four Quartets, "Little Gidding," Section V

We have inherited a fascinating chapter of human exploration that stands on the shoulders of a rich history and a history-in-the-making. Since returning to operation, the space shuttle has continued to perform well, delivering much of the rest of the ISS to orbit, including laboratory modules from the European Space Agency and Japan. The ISS has all of the international partners represented and operating on orbit. All the control centers around the world are running around the clock. International participation among the expeditions has continued to grow to include those from all of the partner astronaut corps. The Station is now occupied with a full complement of six crew members. The ISS program continues to execute a growing scope of scientific research as it transitions from the assembly phase to full utilization.

168

Only history will tell the full benefits of the current chapter of space exploration. All of the implications and impacts on the future are impossible to predict. Whatever the results, the benefits will come only because of the hard work and dedication by the untold—and largely unknown—people who have dedicated their lives toward expanding the frontier. Along the way, there will be periods when we take for granted the progress made. At times, our fortitude will be tested with challenges and setbacks. But we will pass the tests and press on.

Our bigger challenge is not technical, but rather to stay the course of the vision. As countries and cultures, the half-life of our attention span is short. We lose interest quickly. Our memory of whcrc wc have come from—our history—is easily lost. All of that makes us susceptible to losing sight of the vision of exploration and discovery. The vision not only includes destinations but journeys. Those journeys will take us to places of discovery, but they will also nourish our appreciation for what we already have. The ongoing journey will also inspire the next generation and beyond toward countless other destinations, both on and off the planet. **The journey continues.**

Afterword

When Martin Luther was working out the doctrine of vocation, he was, of course, thinking of farmers and merchants, milkmaids and dukes, not astronauts. And yet, Luther, like us, lived in an age in which new worlds were discovered and explored.

The word *astronaut* comes from the Greek word for "sailor" combined with the Greek word for "star," so that an astronaut is someone who sails to the stars. Sailors to the New World, like astronauts today, embarked on long, dangerous, and complex missions. When Luther was nine years old, Christopher Columbus discovered for Europeans "the New World." The very existence of a vast land in the Western Hemisphere astounded the Europeans. The Americas were full of exotic natural landscapes, strange-seeming civilizations, and alien life forms (previously unknown species of animals and plants), so that the New World might just as well have been another planet.

According to Luther, God assigns or stations His redeemed children to places or positions of service. He then calls them to those assignments. "Only let each person lead the life that the Lord has assigned to him, and to which God has called him" (1 Corinthians 7:17). A Christian has multiple vocations—literally, a calling—in the human estates that God has founded: the Church, into which we have been called "by the Gospel" (Third Article, Meaning, *Luther's Small Catechism with Explanation*); the family, with its vocations of husband and wife, father and mother, parent and child; the workplace, in which we exercise our God-given gifts and opportunities; and the state, the culture and community in which we live and interact with others.

The purpose of every vocation—at church, in the home, on the job, in the culture, and, presumably, in outer space—is to love and serve our neighbors. God does not need our good works, said Luther, stressing that our relationship to Him is based solely on the grace and forgiveness we find in the crucified and resurrected Christ. Our neighbor, however, does need our good works. We are justified by faith in Christ, who then sends us out to live out our faith in love and service to our neighbor, something that primarily happens in our diverse vocations.

So where do we see vocation in this book of high-tech adventure, out-of-this-world exploration, and dazzling photographs?

Col. Williams experienced some of the most awe-inspiring sights that any human being has ever witnessed. But unlike nature mystics and subjectivist romantics, he does not confuse them with God. He states that the way to know God is through the even more overwhelming Word of Christ. Col. Williams is a man who hears God's calling in the language of God's Word. He sees the universe and its vastness, with the earth and its intricate magnificence, as the mere "fringes" of God's majesty, His good and reliable and wonderful creation that can be no rival to its Creator. More than that, he recognizes that even the Creation and the transcendent God who made it are of little help apart from the revelation in that Word that God became flesh, entering His creation from an astounding height, to empty Himself, to suffer, to die as an atonement for our sins, and to be raised for our salvation.

Col. Williams is also a family man. His career has often taken him away from his family, but his thoughts are always with them. While he is weightless and hurtling thousands of miles per hour in outer space, he is always thinking of home, eagerly reading his wife's messages and poignantly looking down on their hometown of Houston.

In his vocation in the workplace—the International Space Station hurtling through space—we see Col. Williams at work. He performs his tasks—from mastering the techniques of space flight to tidying up the living space, from executing complex experiments to repairing broken equipment, even when this means leaving the spacecraft and "walking" in outer space—with cool professionalism. The gift to be an astronaut has been given to Col. Williams by God.

Col. Williams also exercises his calling in the state. He is a soldier—one of the few Army officers, a helicopter pilot, to make it as an astronaut—and he serves his country without complaint. Most of us would probably resist being separated from our families, but Col. Williams, "a man under authority" (Matthew 8:9), serves where he is stationed, even, literally, at a space station.

But to whom is Col. Williams to be a neighbor during the six months he spends in the isolation of a cold and empty space? He is not by himself. He is accompanied by the Russian cosmonaut Pavel Vinogradov. Consider that when both men were in the earlier stages of their military careers, they were trained to fight each other. The book says nothing about whether they got on each other's nerves. They learned each other's language. They were neighbors of the closest kind. Later, they were joined by Thomas Reiter, a German, whose immediate ancestors warred with both Russia and the United States. Here we see vocation in its depths. Jesus tells us not only to love our neighbors but to love our enemies. Presumably, the way to do that is to turn them into our neighbors. And that seemed to happen in the close confines of an orbiting spacecraft.

We, too, have now become Col. Williams' neighbors. His feeling that he had a responsibility to convey to other people what he experienced in space motivated him to take up the camera so that others could see what he was seeing. Thus, in the pages of this book, as he tells his story and shows us his photographs, he is loving and serving us.

God Himself works in and through our vocations—providing daily bread through farmers and bakers; creating new life through mothers and fathers; protecting us through policemen, firemen, and the legal system; healing us through doctors and nurses; creating beauty through artists; giving us the blessings of technology through scientists and engineers. Vocation, said Luther, is a mask of God, who, as Col. Williams says, is "hidden" in the world He providentially governs.

Luther would certainly see being an astronaut as a vocation from God.

Gene Edward Veith

About the Photographs

The index that follows includes all of the photographs used within the pages of this book in the order presented. The vast majority are earth observation images taken by Jeff Williams from the International Space Station during Expedition 13. Those images are used courtesy of the Image Science & Analysis Laboratory, NASA Johnson Space Center. They can be accessed on The Gateway to Astronaut Photography of Earth Web site at http://eol.jsc.nasa.gov. Most of the flight photography was taken using the Kodak Professional DCS 760C digital camera using lenses of various focal lengths up to 800mm. Several were taken using the Nikon F5 35mm film camera. The specific camera and lens data along with the ISS location for each photo are available on the Web site.

Photos not found on The Gateway to Astronaut Photography site can be accessed from NASA's Space Station Gallery Web site at http://spaceflight.nasa.gov/gallery/images/station/ either directly or by request.

All images on the Web sites are in the public domain. They are freely available from NASA using the unique identifying photo number included in the index that follows.